GRETCHEN MORGAN

Foreword by Yong Zhao

innovative educators

AN **ACTION PLAN** FOR TEACHERS

HEINEMANN
Portsmouth, NH

Heinemann

361 Hanover Street

Portsmouth, NH 03801–3912

www.heinemann.com

Offices and agents throughout the world

The author and publisher wish to thank those who have generously given permission to reprint borrowed material:

Tony Wagner quotes from the article "Need a Job? Invent It" by Thomas L. Friedman. Published in the *New York Times* Sunday Review, The Opinion Pages, March 30, 2013. Reprinted by permission of Tony Wagner.

Credits continue on page x.

Library of Congress Cataloging-in-Publication Data

Morgan, Gretchen.

   Innovative educators : an action plan for teachers / Gretchen Morgan ; foreword by Yong Zhao.

      pages cm.

   Includes bibliographical references.

   ISBN: 978-0-325-06081-1

   1. Teaching. 2. Creative thinking. 3. Educational innovations. 4. Education—Study and teaching.

5. Teacher effectiveness. I. Title.

LB1027.M617 2014

371.102—dc23   2014024937

Editor: Margaret LaRaia

Production: Victoria Merecki

Cover design: Suzanne Heiser

Cover images: © koosen/Shutterstock; © Lyudmyla Kharlamora/Shutterstock; © tanewpix/Shutterstock

Interior design: Joyce Weston

Typesetter: Gina Poirier, Gina Poirier Design

Manufacturing: Steve Bernier

Printed in the United States of America on acid-free paper

18 17 16 15 14 VP 1 2 3 4 5

Contents

Foreword by Yong Zhao   v

Acknowledgments   viii

1. Introduction: Being Proactive Is More Important Now Than Ever   1

2. The Mindset and Rationale for Intellectual Risk-Taking   21

3. What Is a Responsible Innovation Process?   32

Process of Responsible Innovation

4. Identify the Problem and Problem-Solving Strategy   42

5. Plan   51

6. Implement, Monitor, Analyze, and Share   68

7. When Should You Convert Existing Practices?   74

8. When Should You Invent New Practices?   98

9. Calling All Teachers   104

Appendix: Responsible Innovation Process in Full   107

References   117

Foreword

We are well aware that our children will live in a world drastically different from the world we inhabited in the past and the one we inhabit at present. We are also well aware that today's education is inadequate for preparing our children to live successfully and happily in this new world. But when it comes to what needs to be done, opinions vary.

The dominant view, as reflected in the major reform efforts undertaken in the United States over the past few decades, is that we need to continue to do what we have been doing, just do it better: design better curriculum and establish higher standards for all students (centrally prescribe what each and every child should learn, as exemplified by the Common Core State Standards); prepare better, harder-working teachers and school leaders (establish tougher accountability measures for teachers and principals, as exemplified by No Child Left Behind and Race to the Top); create better assessments and make data-driven decisions (deliver and manage uniform standardized testing via modern technologies, as exemplified by mandating common assessments and pushing for Big Data).

However, this view is fundamentally flawed and results in futile, even counterproductive actions that waste precious resources and squander opportunities. The fixes, no matter how successful, simply reinforce an outdated paradigm; we need a new paradigm that can equip our children with an entirely different set of skills, perspectives, capabilities, and understandings. Doing the wrong thing "right" will not bring the desired outcomes.

The biggest flaw of the dominant view is its failure to recognize that the inadequacy of today's education lies in its design. The paradigm that governs today's schooling was designed for a different society, one that required similar basic cognitive skills and knowledge for routine assembly-line jobs in geographically and culturally isolated communities. All the proposed fixes can only make traditional schooling more effective in producing outdated skills that are of little value in the new society.

Changes brought about over the past few decades by globalization and technology have created a new world in which we consume more personalized, psychological, and spiritual products and services. The skills we need require critical thinking, teamwork, problem solving, creativity, analytic reasoning, and communication (in Daniel Pink's iteration: design, story, symphony, empathy, play, and meaning). We also need to be able to live, interact, and work with people across national and cultural borders. Furthermore, to compete with machines, we must have well-developed "noncognitive" skills that are uniquely human: grit, hope, perseverance, open-mindedness, social adeptness, and emotional intelligence.

The new education has to value individual differences, celebrate diversity, and follow children's passion and interest. It should proceed from the belief that all children have the potential to become great in their own way. It needs to change from fixing children's deficits as measured against preconceived standards to supporting their individual strengths. It needs to become personalized, not nationally or globally standardized.

In this refreshing book Gretchen Morgan speaks out for the new education. She offers compelling evidence showing why the traditional "factory" schools cannot adequately prepare students for the new society. More important, as a former principal, Gretchen understands schools and schooling extremely well. Her extensive experiences in the trenches and acute analytical skills led her to the insight that the factory school breeds a culture that has little chance of encouraging innovation:

> In the last hundred years of refining and reforming factory school, we have become incredibly good at teaching our children to be passive. Factory school has also been pretty effective at encouraging teachers to adopt passive dispositions. This is where the ineffective idea of fidelity has its roots. If the archetype of the American teacher was built on the archetype of the American factory worker, then it was built to implement ideas rather than create them. It was also built to operate with a sense of distrust in management. This results in a culture of compliance and oversight rather than empowerment and innovation.

To change the culture, to move away from schooling's factory disposition, we must have innovative teachers. Gretchen has faith, lots of it, in teachers as the driving force for bringing about the new education we need:

- Teachers need responsible ways to innovate in service of helping all students become proactive learners, professionals, and community members.

- Teachers can both convert existing practices and invent new ways of teaching in an effort to help individual students realize their unique potential.

- Teachers are creative, dedicated, and crafty professionals who can quickly try, fail, succeed, learn, and collectively work together to redesign the way we do school.

Her faith is coupled with suggestions that can help teachers become innovative in their practice, suggestions rooted in her own experiences leading innovations in schools and in current research about innovative teaching, not wishful prescriptions or personal reflections. These suggestions are accessibly—and beautifully—presented as a series of conversations with teachers. I know you will enjoy these conversations as much as I have.

Yong Zhao

Presidential Chair and Director of the Institute for Global and Online Education, College of Education, University of Oregon
Author of *World Class Learners: Educating Creative and Entrepreneurial Students*

Acknowledgments

I think the best reason to write a book is that doing so may inspire and help others to do great stuff. But I have discovered that one of the best selfish parts of writing this book is that it gives me an opportunity to publicly thank really fantastic people. I am the product of an amazing community of thinkers, doers, champions, ancestors, and friends. I cannot overstate how blessed I have been each day of my life by the powerful people who surround me.

First, to Mom and Dad. I have never had a winning lottery ticket, or won a raffle, and the only Bingo prize I have ever taken home was a weird little rug depicting a scene of lions lounging on a hot day, but that has never bothered me because I believe it is a tradeoff for the big lottery win of being given to the two of you. Now that I am a parent myself, it is clear to me just how hard the two of you worked to teach me to try, to care, to believe, to learn, and to do important and helpful things. Thanks.

To Stephen, or as you are more commonly known, Sweetie Morgan. You are one of the few people who really knows how much writing this book both scared me and meant to me. Thanks for the encouragement, the time to write, the spontaneous foot rubs, and the timely delivery of so many extra hot soy chai beverages. Besides being a wonderful father and teacher, you are an amazing husband who often notices before I do that I am out of whack and offers me just the right support before I know I need it. You are simply wonderful. I love you like crazy.

To Henry and Sylvie—you two are amazing. Thanks for knowing just when to crawl in and sever the connection between my lap and my laptop, putting an end to my writing and initiating much-needed cuddles. I learn from the two of you every day. You are both blessed with wonderful little minds and strong hearts. The very best part of my life is watching you grow and learning more and more about who you are and who you will be. Love you more than anything.

To the teachers featured in this book, Heather, Sonia, Paul, and Liza. And to the other teachers I interviewed, but whose content didn't end up in the final book: Scott, Bethanne, and Chad. To all of you, thanks for sharing your thinking and asking great questions. But mostly, thanks for the work you do for the kids in your care. I have had moments in each of your rooms when you did something so beautiful and clever that all I could do was stop, watch, and smile.

Thanks to Sam Bennett for taking me out for sushi and getting me into this mess, and equal thanks to Margaret LaRaia for riding along through the couple years it took to organize my messy mind and produce this thing.

Thanks also to those of you both brave and kind enough to read this and talk to me about this while it was still a complicated mess and helped me sort it out—thanks to Jen, Furman, Sam, Colleen, and Ken.

Thanks to Yong Zhao. Reading *World Class Learners* inspired me to keep writing. You helped me see the broader context in which my thinking made sense. Thank you for your global perspective, for introducing me to entrepreneurial indicators, and for the lovely foreword you wrote for this book. I feel I should also personally thank you for the idea that our school system should aspire to keep kids from wanting to graduate and live in their parents' basement. I always credit you when I share that simple measure of systemic success or failure with friends at dinner parties.

Thanks to the long list of my dear colleagues from TC, RMSEL, EL Schools, Venture Prep, and the Colorado Department of Education . . . you taught me how to collaborate. You taught me how to make my actions and words intentionally mirror my beliefs about kids. You challenged my limitations and expected me to always grow and do better. We have done absolutely crazy amazing things together in service of lighting up the kids in our classrooms. Thanks for inquiring, integrating, writing, sailing, building, facilitating, designing, starting, stopping, and trying so many fantastic things together. I hope you can each recognize the bits I learned from you and tried to put to good use in the pages that follow.

And to those of you who were my students, big thanks for helping me build a loud, inventive, messy, fast-paced, creative, and collaborative classroom. You remain some of my most powerful teachers.

Who knew that a girl who is 80 percent head, 15 percent stomach, and 5 percent heart would be so gushy?

g.

Credits continued from page ii:

Introduction

Being Proactive Is More Important Now Than Ever

Hi there. We don't know each other, but I hope we are about to have some great conversations. Before we begin, I want you to know what I am hoping to do and why I wrote this book. (Please don't turn the page. This isn't personal blather important for me to write down but irrelevant to you as a reader; that stuff was part of the acknowledgments.) To increase the chances that you and I are able to communicate effectively in this somewhat limited medium, I am trying to be clear about my goals and intentions so you can use that information as you read what follows. I normally rely on flailing my hands around and making cartoon faces to convey meaning. Unable to do that here, I'm going with clarity of intention.

Redefining the Relationship Between Fidelity and Innovation

In many ways writing this book allows me to revisit a failure from my time as a principal. I was trying to guide the school by taking a clear, shared approach to instruction because my colleagues and I believed that consistency in the learning environment was good for students (I still believe this). At the same time, I wanted our school to continue to innovate. Without a process to support innovation, however, ideas came in fits and starts and weren't explored in an organized way. It was left to me to become a kind of dictator who decided whether we should or shouldn't do something different. This experience taught me two things:

1. I don't want to be a dictator. I don't like the wardrobe, the required demeanor, or the idea that one person should be the decider.

2. Without some process inviting people to innovate we would always have a destructive dynamic between rogue actors and rule followers on our staff.

We were struggling with the commonly held false dichotomy that fidelity and innovation don't mix. I offer the counter idea that mixing innovation and fidelity is required if schools are to serve students effectively over time. Organized and intentional innovation is essential in determining what everyone should start or stop implementing with fidelity in a school that evolves in response to changes in society.

Currently, we use the idea of fidelity to measure the degree to which we are implementing something as it was originally intended, to be able to determine whether it works in a new setting. For example, when a new reading program is adopted, there are often people paid to travel from room to room around the district observing to see whether this new approach is being implemented with fidelity. In this case, we are supposed to have fidelity to rote and inflexible implementation of a program or tool.

This vision of fidelity is in direct conflict with innovation. It assumes that innovation does and should happen outside the school and be brought inside the school to be implemented. This kind of fidelity of implementation is intended to ensure consistency for students and contain the risk of having bad teachers. I would argue that this approach is actually not very good at limiting the negative impact of bad teachers, but it is very good at limiting the positive impact of good teachers.

So instead, I am suggesting that we need to think of innovation as the responsibility of teachers. We need teachers to be proactive problem solvers, continually analyzing the effectiveness of current strategies and innovating to meet the rapidly changing task of educating our children in the twenty-first century. However, we also need to organize the practice of innovating so it isn't just something that individual teachers do for their individual learning and for the benefit of the thirty students in their classroom. We need to organize our efforts so that we can collectively, and based on sound practices, determine what should be implemented with fidelity across part or all of the school in service of all students getting access to our collective best practice.

To help equip educators for this conversation, let's examine where the idea of American public education started and what it has become.

How the History of Public Education Informs Our Present

Public education became a national phenomenon in 1918 when all states at last had mandatory attendance laws requiring and providing at least an elementary education (Watson 2008). At that time our predecessors established the basic structures and systems of the American schoolhouse. They built it by mimicking common aspects of adult life at the time. This seemed like a good idea. Our public school system began at the height of the industrial revolution, and the factory was the new engine of the economy and in many ways the culture. There were large numbers of immigrant children in urban centers, and schools were asked to prepare them for jobs in the "new" economy (Roundtable, Inc. 2001).

The story of the American schoolhouse through the rest of the twentieth century is a blurred series of pendulum swings, periods of fifteen to twenty years in which progressive ideas gained momentum followed by fifteen to twenty years that emphasized tracking and basic skills. Somewhat surprisingly, very little has changed in the way schools are organized, led, and managed. With some interesting exceptions, most schools have been run like factories. Both students and teachers work within rigid systems designed to sort and classify, and schools are still primarily managed through compliance.

Factory School = Factory Disposition = Passive Disposition

Whether students are deeply engaged or totally disengaged in school, we do a pretty good job of teaching them to take on a factory disposition. Even if students find themselves at odds with the way things work—when we ask them to pretend they don't have access to knowledge on their smart phones or try to convince them that writing revisions by hand is a great use of their time—they learn that being quiet and waiting is a pretty good way to make it through. Our system takes kids with a range of passive or proactive dispositions and teaches them all to "get in line." American schools exert a lot of energy teaching students:

- How to raise their hand and be called on before they speak

- How to follow procedures when bells ring or lights are turned off-and-on

- That when they do what they are asked, they get candy (or stickers or extra recess)

- How to hold their questions until there is a break in the lecture

- Not talk to another student if you need help but to raise your hand and wait for the teacher.

In the last hundred years of refining and reforming factory school, we have become incredibly good at teaching our children to be passive. Factory school has also been pretty effective at encouraging teachers to adopt passive dispositions. This is where the ineffective idea of fidelity has its roots. If the archetype of the American teacher was built on the archetype of the American factory worker, then it was built to implement ideas, rather than create them. It was also built to operate with a sense of distrust in management. This results in a culture of compliance and oversight, rather than empowerment and innovation.

In recent years, driven by a well-intentioned equity agenda and wanting to make up for the years of learning that students didn't get while they were not engaged or instruction wasn't effective, schools across the country are trying to maximize the academic-skill-building potential of every minute of every day. To gain efficiency, some of these schools have taken compliance to an extreme. Clearly, efficient use of time is important, and wasting kids' time is irresponsible. But is giving students small opportunities to manage their own time or behavior in less constrained and explained environments a waste of time? More to the point, how will children ever learn to manage time, prioritize, or demonstrate initiative when every minute of the day is so tightly controlled?

This is not to endorse swinging the pendulum all the way to days filled with two-hour unstructured "work time" but rather to request that we balance compliance with social norms and efficiency with the explicit development of a proactive disposition. Reading gains or not, in too many American schools, we teach our children to behave in a way that produces diligent but passive people, which ultimately may make them unemployable as twenty-first-century professionals.

In the last twenty-five years, a desire to ensure both equity and global competitiveness has resulted in significant changes in policy regarding student assessment and school accountability. Those policies effectively changed the mission of public education from measuring and sorting students to measuring students and then attempting to provide varied means of support so that all students leave the schoolhouse with the same basic competencies. As a nation we have committed to not leaving any child behind, and in doing so we have redefined equity in the context of the American schoolhouse.

When we began standardized testing, it revealed dramatic inequities in achievement. Educators and policymakers could no longer say that American education was providing equal opportunity just by offering free access to a school in every community. As a result, the focus has shifted to making sure every school in every community provides a *quality* education to all of the children it serves. We have committed to all students achieving common standards, gaining the same set of skills and knowledge. We have made a concerted effort to address these inequities and have made some progress toward closing performance gaps:

- The NAEP assessment began in the 1970s and is given to a sample of students ages nine, thirteen, and seventeen throughout the country every two to four years. If you compare scores from the early 1970s and 2012, in most areas overall scores are going up and the gaps in performance that exist between ethnic groups are slowly narrowing (National Center for Education Statistics 2013).

- The gap in the dropout rate between high-income and low-income families narrowed between 1970 and 2011, particularly during the past two decades, when the gap narrowed from 21 percentage points in 1990 to 11 percentage points in 2011 (Aud et al. 2013a).

However, the data also indicate that we are still some distance from closing achievement gaps:

- We continue to see significant gaps in high school graduation rates. In 2010, the white-black gap in high school graduation rates was 17 percentage points and the white-Hispanic gap was 12 percentage points (Aud et al. 2013a).

- The gap between college graduation rates of minority and white first-time, full-time degree seekers has basically been flat, with a slight overall increase from the cohort who entered college in 1996 to the cohort who entered in 2006 (Snyder and Dillow 2012).

While we have certainly made some progress with leading indicators like K–12 literacy and math performance, the college graduation rate indicates that these gains in a narrow set of academic measures are not increasing postsecondary success. Additionally, these hard-earned test results have come at a cost. As we drove hard for equality in our system, we decided that helping all students develop the same set of knowledge and skills was so important that other types of learning could be ignored. This belief has resulted in a number of tradeoffs. Art, music, and fitness programs have been cut in favor of additional literacy or math instruction. In my home state, Colorado, many elementary schools stopped teaching social studies a decade ago because it wasn't tested. Missing out on social studies, art, music, or fitness is cause for concern.

However, these tradeoffs also need to be examined in another context. As education reform focused on the implementation of better standards and assessments, societal, economic, and labor arenas were experiencing dramatic change responding to, and capitalizing on, the blazing speed of technological innovation.

We had no idea twenty-five years ago that YouTube and Facebook would empower social revolutions or imperil naïve adolescents. Unlike teachers in the early twentieth century, we don't know what jobs to prepare children for; many of the jobs that will exist ten or twenty years from now haven't yet been imagined. Who knew in the '90s that being a social media manager would be a high-paying job today? And even with regard to jobs that are likely to continue, being a doctor for example, we cannot imagine *how* people will be doing those jobs. Doctors twenty years ago had no idea they would routinely be able to use tools like three-dimensional imaging or genetic testing to diagnose patients.

The number of fields in which basic skills and a high school diploma alone make a person a powerful contributor are dwindling. This is happening for two reasons: There are fewer manufacturing jobs, and there are large numbers of college graduates (48 percent in 2013) competing for jobs that do not require a college degree (Vedder, Denhart, and Robe 2013). And on the contrary, being able to access and synthesize learning from the Internet and knowing how to utilize the Internet's powerful communication potential can make an employee a real asset.

In a recent interview in the *New York Times*, Tony Wagner, an education professor at Harvard, said, "Because knowledge is available on every Internet-connected device, what you know matters far less than what you can do with what you know. The capacity to innovate—the ability to solve problems creatively or bring new possibilities to life—and skills like critical thinking, communication, and collaboration are far more important than academic knowledge. . . . Young people who are intrinsically motivated—curious, persistent, and willing to take risks—will learn new knowledge and skills continuously. They will be able to find new opportunities or create their own—a disposition that will be increasingly important as many traditional careers disappear" (Friedman 2013). Wagner is describing a proactive disposition, something our schools, built to mimic factories, were not built to foster.

If you or someone you're trying to convince needs more outside data, consider the Conference Board's 2006 survey of 431 employers, from across different fields and who hire people with varying levels of education, about the skills they believed were most important for new hires to be successful in their industry. The following graph shows in order of least to most important (top to bottom) what those employers said. Let's see how their findings compare to the themes you identified from talking to people across other industries (see Figure 1.1).

The bottom line is that, independent of the industry our students want to join, all students now need capacity beyond basic skills. Students need to grow up to be creative, socially responsible, critical-thinking, problem-solving, collaborative, and hard-working professionals.

The Balance of Fidelity and Innovation in Practice

Reform hasn't fallen short as the result of a lack of effort; the problem has been direction. Exerting tremendous effort, keeping noses to the grindstone, has made it difficult to notice that the context around public education was changing. We've been reforming to address social inequity within the context of the past, not the present or the future. To keep up with the speed of change, we need to renovate the American schoolhouse so that it meets today's needs. This doesn't mean creating an ugly hodgepodge of additions—given how much we have already tried to jam into and add to our existing structure, which no longer has time for social studies or art, it isn't feasible to adopt new programs and introduce a "proactive class." There literally isn't time in the day or year. Instead, we have to think about strengthening and reviving the basic design, so that it meets today's context. That doesn't mean that our reform efforts have been a failure. The redefinition of equity would not have been possible without clear standards and recent reform efforts. And it is essential that we carry that commitment to serving each student well with us as we take these next steps.

Even if it were practical, adding on classes to learn how to be proactive wouldn't be an effective way to teach students to adopt a proactive disposition. We didn't have a "factory class" to teach our students to become passive factory employees; we

Figure 1.1   Results from 2006 Conference Board Survey of 431 Employers

This graphic representation created by the Center for Public Education to summarize findings in the original Conference Board report. http://www.centerforpubliceducation.org/Learn-About/21st-Century/Defining-a-21st-Century-Education-Full-Report-PDF.pdf, page 47

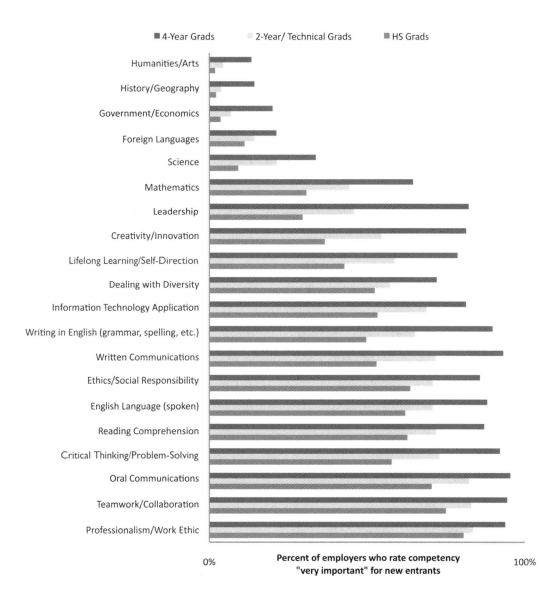

Partnership for 21st Century Skills, The Conference Board, Corporate Voices for Working Families, and Society for Human Resource Management (2006). *Are They Really Ready to Work?* Washington, DC. Categories are ranked according to the average of the three bars.

designed school to mimic the factory. There is so much power in routines, language, expectations, and ritual. These are our best tools to teach students what kinds of behavior are desirable. To realign school to the twenty-first century, we need to be willing to reimagine completely the look, feel, and structure of the American schoolhouse. Reimagining doesn't mean that we need to discard everything. Like a good home renovator, we can design new things while also finding new uses for the old, beautiful, and familiar things.

We need to use both conversion and invention to redesign all aspects of school, from management practices to culture to instruction to routines to curriculum to technology use, so that they mimic the current and emerging society and economy. We also need to redesign our schoolhouse to be flexible—to mimic the quickly evolving vision of adult life. We need to imagine something less like factory school and more like Google school. Many other educators have used comparisons with Google to inspire conversations about the future of school. I like them as a case-study because Google grew up in the twenty-first century and has one of the most future-looking approaches to business. We should look as far forward as possible. Google has changed the way leaders interact with contributors, the way work is organized, what it means to specialize, and how to value creation and innovation while still getting things done.

Consider Google's hiring practices. In an interview with the *New York Times* Laszlo Bock, senior vice president of people operations, described what they've learned from carefully mining data about job applicants' characteristics and their resulting performance.

- In some teams at Google, 14 percent of people don't have a college degree.
- GPA and test scores are not good predictors of job performance at Google.

If students' ability to do well in school is not a predictor of their ability to work well at Google, then our school system doesn't have priorities aligned to the emerging modern economy.

- The head of people operations at Google thinks that people who succeed in college are conditioned to behave in a way that inhibits their potential to do well at Google.

Students need to be comfortable undertaking legitimate inquiry. Teaching real inquiry is challenging but not because kids aren't naturally curious or are unwilling to persist in the face of ambiguity. Teaching inquiry is difficult because we have taught students, K–12 and postsecondary, that their job as learners is to build and demonstrate a body of fixed knowledge and discrete skills. We could go a long way toward building people who like "figuring out stuff" if we just teach students that knowledge and skills are important not in themselves but because we need them to analyze, reason, and synthesize, which is the real work of a learner.

Avinash Kaushik worked for Google as a digital marketing contractor for eleven months. In an entry on his blog, *Occam's Razor*, he listed ten things he learned about Google during his time there. Here's number five:

> **Empowerment (the big small company)**
>
> If you are good at something, have passion to do it, then you'll get empowered to go do it. I know that sounds basic. It is not.
>
> You could be just out of college and if you want to then you'll get to solve some of the most complex challenges you would ever find. At other companies you'll get put into a hierarchy with layers and controls where for the first four years you might learn where all the files are.
>
> I am being a bit dramatic, but not all that much. In my second week there I was walking over to lunch with a young man and he was describing his work to me. He had been at Google for less than a year, straight from college, and had completely rewritten some of the most challenging "code" during the last few months and his work had yielded dramatic results for Google.
>
> He is good at what he does but I was simply struck by how a company this size would allow someone so young and "untested" the task of solving such a complex challenge. And how awesome must it feel to know that you did that!
>
> That's what I mean by empowerment. (Kaushik 2008)

Proactive people in the twenty-first-century workforce aren't limited by hierarchy; they can use their skills and drive to do good work and create interesting opportunities. Innovative educators can take this same stance. When practicing responsible innovation, teachers can make interesting connections and create interesting opportunities for their students, colleagues, and community.

Instead of Fidelity to Programs or Historic Models, Let's Try Belief in People

I wrote this book because I believe in the capability of individuals, and I am worried that the way we currently define the role of teacher, the role of student, and the idea of fidelity is squashing large amounts of that capability. These beliefs underlie the construct of teaching and learning that follows throughout this book.

I want to more fully describe those beliefs here, so we can use them to evaluate ideas throughout the book. Part of being responsible innovators is having a clear rationale for what we do; any rationale for teaching needs to be grounded in what we believe to be true about students. As you read, I invite you to determine how close or far you are from these beliefs and to use alignment with your beliefs as a sort of test to determine when it is time to convert or invent practice in service of doing something better with your students.

Beliefs Teachers Should Share

I wavered a bit on the word choice of this heading. Is "Beliefs Teachers Should Share" too bossy? First, I'm pretty confident that most people reading this book agree. But more importantly, these beliefs are the one thing I feel comfortable being bossy about. There are some objective things we can and should agree upon.

Belief One: All children, no matter where or when they are born, deserve the opportunity to fulfill their potential. While differentiated supports to achieve common outcomes have been the heart of the equity agenda in the last twenty years, equity now means everyone having an equal shot at maximizing their potential. It is essential that we hold onto this belief about equity as we redesign the American schoolhouse.

The result of this belief is that we take on the responsibility to teach all students to be **proactive learners** *who investigate, synthesize, build fluency, analyze connections, self-assess, know themselves well, and consider a range of perspectives.*

When I was a school leader, I worked with our staff to explore this belief. We talked about whether we believed different characteristics of successful adults were innate or learned. We examined, for example, whether each of us were born with, or developed, self-discipline. The general consensus at the end of the activity was that while it was certainly easier for some of us to learn self-discipline than others, we were all able to identify how we *learned* to behave that way. We had all learned self-discipline and other behaviors of successful people basically the same way we learned academic things. It came down to some combination of the following for each of us:

- People modeled self-discipline for us.

- People labeled it when they saw us demonstrate self-discipline.

- Someone expected us to have self-discipline.

- Someone gave us advice and opportunities to practice self-discipline.

- Someone gave us quality feedback about the degree to which we were demonstrating self-discipline.

- There was significant accountability for demonstrating self-discipline.

- We were rewarded for demonstrating self-discipline.

- We were in a situation where self-discipline was of dire importance, so to avoid sinking, we figured it out.

In every teacher-hiring process I have ever been a part of, I have asked people directly about their belief that all children can learn, and how that belief plays out in their classroom on a daily basis. Most applicants describe things they do to offer additional chances, feedback, and additional support to students as they strive to learn a math skill or write a quality essay. Very few people express a belief that they can provide some explicit instruction, feedback, and support to teach a lazy or unorganized kid how to be productive or keep their stuff together.

What Does Proactive Learning Look Like?

My eight-year-old son is deeply fascinated with birds, especially raptors. This fascination has led our entire family to be proactive learners. We have a desperate need, whenever we are outside, to identify every bird we see. Bird identification is a sophisticated application of both knowledge and skills. In our early stages as "birders" we tried to be good at identifying despite our shallow knowledge base and lack of detailed observation skills. Not surprisingly, we were not good at identifying birds. We might have, upon spotting a brown bird, suggested that we were seeing: a kestrel, a prairie falcon, or a barn swallow.

See Figure 1.2 (photos inserted at approximate scale) to understand how lame our bird identification skills were.

Thankfully, we disagreed frequently enough about what we each thought we were seeing that it was easy for each of us to acknowledge that at least some of us didn't know what we were talking about.

Figure 1.2 Kestrel, Barn Swallow, Prairie Falcon

This awareness caused us to feel a real need to build some knowledge and practice some skills. Since our humble beginnings, we have gone to a local nature center, and events held by raptor rescue organizations, to listen to lectures from experts. We have read no fewer than forty books and studied bird identification cards for birds in our region. We have practiced watching birds closely, so we know now that good birders use more than color to identify birds. Wing shape, type of flight, size and shape of tail feathers, head shape, relative size, and speed can all be used to help identify the bird. With more knowledge and greater skill, we have become respectable birders.

Our family has done just what children need to learn to do. We discovered a curiosity, and in trying to pursue that curiosity, we identified that we didn't know much and weren't very good at it. We then accessed information from a broad range of sources. As we gathered information, we paid close attention to patterns and effective strategies, and we independently learned and applied new information.

To go a bit deeper into the idea of a proactive learner—I want you to come back in time to when I was in elementary school. I wish I was about to tell you that my elementary school years were a great example of what we *can* do to help students learn how to be proactive learners. Sadly, it will be the counterexample.

What follows is a comparison of my experience in elementary school and what I hope my children will experience now. I want to be very clear that I do not assume that we have all had the same experiences or received all of these messages as children when we were in school. I do suspect, however, that we have something in common in our experience and that some of those commonalities, some of the underpinnings of factory school and the factory disposition we were taught in school, no longer align with the realities of adult life.

	What I learned in my K–12 experience in the 20th century	What I hope my kids will experience as students in the 21st century (as far as we can tell)
What are the shared societal values related to education, opportunity, and how work is done?	• Everyone should have an equal opportunity. • College is the pathway to professional work and career advancement. • Roles at work are sorted into blue collar and white collar. • Hierarchy and experience are deeply valued.	• Individuals are different from one another and have unique talents. • Being entrepreneurial is as important, if not more, than college as a pathway to career advancement. • There is a growing creative class of employee; their collars vary in color. • Good ideas are deeply valued and invited from people at all levels of an organization.

| *What skills do students need to develop to be competent adults in that society?* | • Ability to follow directions
• Willingness to follow rigid schedules
• Ability to memorize information and multi-step processes
• Understand hierarchy: be polite/patient and wait for someone to notice your good work, and you will receive opportunities
• Desire to do your best and work hard | • Ability to formulate, organize, and communicate your original ideas
• Ability to manage your time
• Ability to independently evaluate, learn, synthesize, and use new information
• Willingness to speak up and promote your ideas and advocate for yourself
• Desire to do your best combined with a desire to work both hard and smart |

To help illustrate what I believe is the key difference, I created lists below of all of the verbs I used to describe my experience (on the left) and what our students need now (on the right).

The column describing my elementary school experience includes the following verbs:		The column describing the emerging vision of the 21st century includes the following verbs:	
• Follow	• Wait	• Formulate	• Use
• Memorize	• Receive	• Organize	• Speak Up
• Understand	• Do	• Communicate	• Promote
• Be	• Work Hard	• Manage	• Do
		• Learn	• Work Hard and Smart
		• Synthesize	

If you close your eyes and imagine a student doing all the things in the left column, what do you see? I see a six-year-old me, happy and quiet and sitting in my desk with nothing in my hands. I see me watching the teacher closely, and I see me nodding my head a lot. I see me alone at my desk with a workbook and pencil trying to do my best and work my fastest, looking up to see if anyone else finishes before me. I see me nonchalantly smearing thin layers of Elmer's white glue on my left palm to make fake skin to keep from getting in trouble for talking as I waited for everyone to finish their workbook page so we could get our next directions. The verbs in this list are passive, and, with the exception of working hard, this image of me as a student is also *passive*.

Now close your eyes and imagine a student doing the things in the twenty-first-century column. Imagine a student formulating, speaking up, and promoting. Are they sitting down? Are they quiet? Are they focused exclusively on the teacher? Do they have time to perfect the process of using Elmer's white glue to create fake skin? I don't think so.

I think they are on the edge of their seat and leaning over their table full of work. I think they are talking to other students and listening to other students. I think they are writing things down and trying to put their ideas together into words and pictures so they can figure something out. I think they are frequently both curious and frustrated. I think they see their teacher as an advisor and call upon them frequently to bounce ideas off of or get help with something that isn't making sense. The verbs in this list are active, and this student is *proactively learning*.

Beliefs Teachers Should Share

Belief Two: People learn behaviors and ways of thinking and being through persistent clarity of expectation, modeling, practice, and feedback. As described in the introduction, we didn't have "factory class" and we shouldn't have "professional class" or "twenty-first-century class." It is both impractical and ineffective.

The result of this belief is that we redesign the most basic and core characteristics of how we do school so that we use our routines and expectations to foster in all students a disposition of being **proactive professionals** *who adapt, produce, organize, capitalize on connections, learn from failure, manage risk, communicate, promote ideas, and collaborate.*

In his book *World Class Learners*, Yong Zhao refers to a range of entrepreneurial behaviors and a range of entrepreneurs. One such category of new entrepreneurs is called intrapreneurs (Zhao 2012). These are people who behave in entrepreneurial ways as they work inside companies owned and run by other people. I think this is a good way to think about proactive professionals.

Proactive professionals look for connections and opportunities. They are willing to try things when they have some of the skills they need, trusting themselves to build the rest as they go. Proactive professionals speak up and promote ideas. Knowing that not all of their ideas will be great, they are still willing to put good ideas out there to see where they can go. Proactive professionals know their strengths and are good at identifying the strengths of others. They use that self-knowledge and awareness of others to engage in strong, effective collaboration.

It is worth noting that many people also apply their proactive professional capacity to personal or societal endeavors. Maybe despite the fact that a person is a runner and has never been a swimmer, he decides to try to become a triathlete. Or maybe not knowing really how a person goes about it, she organizes her community to build a bike park, gather food for a local food bank, or plant trees. Being a proactive professional is required for a person to do good and important things with the knowledge and skills he or she gains as a proactive learner.

> ## Beliefs Teachers Should Share
>
> **Belief Three: Our democratic society needs to produce many more self-sufficient, contributing, and civic-minded adults than those who need support.** Thomas Jefferson said in the 1700s that our democracy requires well-educated and engaged citizens. In these difficult economic times, we can also see this in a very practical manner. We need to have many, many more taxpayers than people who cannot afford to eat, and we need to have compassion and feel some responsibility for our neighbors who are hungry.
>
> *The result of this belief is that we take responsibility for teaching all students to be* **proactive community members** *who think in global, local, and systemic ways, anticipate implications of decisions, and ultimately make decisions that are good for them, their neighbors, and the broader community.*

Being a proactive community member is important all along the scale, from local to global community.

Think about what it means to be a proactive community member in your neighborhood. What qualities do your best neighbors have? In their local community, proactive people think about how their decisions impact their neighbors. Should I throw trash on the ground? Should I look up when I walk to see if there is someone who may need help crossing the street? Should I plug my headphones in tight and avoid interacting with everyone around me? When an issue emerges in my community will I turn a blind eye, or will I get involved to help? When others in my neighborhood accomplish great things, will I celebrate their success or seek to break them down or feel sorry for myself?

Beyond our neighborhoods, how actively should we be involved in our cities, states, or nation? A proactive community member is aware of local, state, and national issues, considers and learns about different perspectives on those issues, and actively advocates for what they think is right through voting, proactive communication, and having their actions match their priorities.

The Earth Guardians are a great example of young people already playing the role of active community members (http://earthguardians.org/index.shtml). They became aware of a number of environmental issues. Despite their age (eight and eleven when I saw them speak and perform) and the overwhelming size of the issues they became aware of—they felt compelled to act. They created an organization that meets weekly to make plans to take on environmental situations in their community. They also tapped into their unique skills and gifts to identify their most effective strategies. For example, they have written and regularly perform a number of rap songs that demonstrate knowledge of the situation and are very persuasive with audiences. My favorite is, "What the Frack?"

These are the kinds of individuals who will be successful in the twenty-first century. They feel committed to their community, are hard-working, and have identified what they are passionate about and use that to direct their energy. These young people have already embraced their role as community leaders. If we foster that behavior in all children, many more of them will grow up to be active community participants and leaders, the kind of engaged citizens the design of our nation depends on.

Beliefs Teachers Should Share

Belief Four: Teachers are creative, clever, and dedicated professionals. I believe that when we remove the complexity and deep thinking from our work, when we try to adopt tips and tricks or write a "teacher proof" curriculum, we fall short of our potential to help each of our students maximize his or her unique capacity. The only way to honor and maximize the potential of individual students is to empower teachers to dig deep into their practice and redesign the way we do school.

This is why this book primarily speaks to, and features the voices of, teachers. I am operating on the belief that teachers need to come to exemplify proactive learning through responsible inquiry and innovation. Teachers need to model being proactive professionals, willing to take the risk of letting their colleagues into their practice. And finally, teachers need to embrace their role as proactive community members willing to implement innovative practices with collective fidelity to create school environments with the highest quality across classrooms.

The potential for students is maximized when teachers embrace these roles in service of students becoming proactive, capable, and happy adults interested in embracing learning as a lifelong endeavor.

Proactive students grow up to be proactive adults. Proactive people learn more, do more, produce more, contribute more, find and create greater opportunities for themselves. I want to pause for a moment and point out that beyond these personal, professional, and economic advantages, there are other benefits to learning how to be a proactive person. This benefit is equally important for both students and teachers. The following highly simplified construct is one I developed based on things I learned from legitimate researchers like Carol Dweck, the author of *Mindset* (2006), esteemed students involved with assessment–for–learning researchers Black and Wiliam, and Rick Stiggins and the other good people at Assessment Training Institute. Among other things, each of these researchers talk about the mindset a person develops toward learning and how that impacts his or her appetite for future learning. Based on their work, and my personal life experience, I have come to believe the following . . .

As they go through life, proactive people say to themselves:

- I know what I am good at, and I know what is difficult for me.
- I know how to recover and learn from mistakes.
- I know that when I try, I sometimes fail but always learn and sometimes succeed.
- I know that success feels good, because I have felt it before.
- I trust my judgment.
- I make choices on purpose and feel responsible for the positive and negative consequences of my choices.
- Some things are beyond my control, but I have a lot of choices and opportunities.

As they go through life, passive people say to themselves:

- I don't feel like I am really great at anything.
- I do anything I can to avoid making mistakes; they are crushing to me.
- I don't want to try my hardest because it makes failure even more painful. I would rather not try, so I expect the failure and can say I didn't really try.
- I don't think too much about what success feels like, because I am so worried about what it feels like to fail.
- I feel like everything just keeps happening to me.
- I don't think my choices matter because all these things beyond my control will get me in the end anyway.
- I don't think my choices or actions contributed to my situation because I have this other person or situation to blame or justify my choices.

In addition to proactive people being more likely to create opportunities for themselves in the twenty-first-century job market, in general, I believe proactive people have an easier time being happy. People are happier when they are living a life they helped to create, rather than one that feels like it is happening to them.

So, while proactive people may struggle and experience frustration as they try to work out things beyond their knowledge or experience, overall, a life lived in a proactive stance will have greater opportunity for both economic success and personal happiness.

How do we get kids there? Right now students come to factory school with varying degrees of proactive or passive behaviors, and we carefully and thoroughly teach them to be more and more passive. The logic follows that we could work with the same set of students, starting with the same range of dispositions, and instead carefully and thoroughly teach them to be *proactive*.

Believing that we can teach students to be proactive learners, professionals, and community members is a big deal. To use the practices discussed later in the book to build proactive people, I think a teacher must at least be able to imagine a circumstance in which a student might be able to learn to behave as a proactive learner, professional, and community member.

What Do We Do When People Don't Share Our Beliefs?

One of the things I have discovered since branching out from my own classroom is that people who work in other industries don't always value learning as a thing unto itself. They are disheartened when their children want to be literature majors in college or take time out from college to explore some corner of the world. Because to many people, education and learning are a means to an end, that end being economic independence. While I certainly want my children to grow up and live somewhere other than my basement,[1] I (and maybe a few of you) are a little offended by this perspective. I became an educator because I believe education is an essential investment in the quality of my community. I wanted to help individual children grow into unique and wonderful adults because that is the responsibility of humanity, not because the telecom industry told me to.

But despite my frustration on this topic, I think it is time to become a little less frustrated and a great deal more proactive, to spend a little less energy feeling good or bad about why others are willing to value or are eager to undermine public education—and strive instead to help more and more people find value in public education as a common good. It may feel especially challenging to engage in this effort now, when many teachers feel devalued and mistrusted in big things, like districtwide curriculums and daily pacing guides, and small things, like telling someone at a dinner party, "I'm a teacher," and hearing, "Oh. You must really love kids" (translation: "Lucky you, you get to play around all day").

Our peers in other professions don't know how complex teaching is. When we say teaching is a craft, people sometimes misunderstand. It isn't a craft in the sense that we start with colorful materials and use them to create something decorative. It is a craft in that it requires craftsmanship—continued reflection, study, attention, and intention—to be done well. Incidentally, it is probably equally true that we don't know how complex *their* jobs are. The difference is we don't assume we can understand their work because we didn't spend thirteen of the first eighteen years of our life experiencing it.

I will confess, there have been times when I have judged and ignored noneducators who expressed oversimplified and unappreciative views of teaching. I've nodded and

---

[1] Credit must be given to Yong Zhao for suggesting that we may want to measure the quality of our education system by determining what percent of students can and choose to live somewhere other than their parents' basement as young adults.

forced a smile and quickly found a reason to walk away feeling arrogant and smug. As the profession experiences intensified scrutiny, many of our most intentional and creative teachers retreat, whether fearfully or smugly, behind their closed classroom door. Some of the best teachers make a concerted effort to keep their good practice a secret because it strays from the daily pacing guide.

It's time to stop subverting the political processes that shape and direct public education and open our classroom doors. It's time to learn about the nature of work in other professions, listen and try to understand the perspectives of people who don't understand our profession, and help everyone outside our classroom see the importance and complexity of our craft.

A Community of Doers

There are some schools around the country that have figured out that factory management isn't working. Success Academy charter schools are one example (http://jobs.successacademies.org/). While there may be some differing views on these schools, especially in the political context of New York City, there is a key idea they have identified and strive to exemplify in the experiences of both students and teachers in their schools that is relevant to understanding twenty-first-century nonfactory school. Rather than prescribing exactly what students and teachers do, they describe their schools like this:

> Visit any of our schools and you'll feel the energy as soon as you walk through the doors. Instead of defining limits, we challenge scholars to approach each day like investigators, explorers, and sleuths—making discoveries that enrich their knowledge of the world.
>
> In fact, we challenge parents, teachers, leaders, and staff members to do the same. The result is a community of doers with deeply held principles by which we strive to adhere. These core beliefs embody our ACTION values, which stand for:
>
> > Agency—We take ownership and responsibility for all we do.
> > Curiosity—We are fueled by wonder and always ask "what if?"
> > Try and Try—We know that success takes elbow grease.
> > Integrity—We are honest, open, and transparent.
> > Others—We look out for each other with respect and support.
> > No Shortcuts—Excellent learning takes time and effort.

Try to imagine schools full of doers. As we go forward doing the good work of converting beautiful old glass doorknobs into coat racks and inventing new kinds of spaces to match new purposes, we need to think of ourselves this way. We, teachers and school leaders, need to take a proactive stance and become communities of doers.

Now is the time for us to tap into our own creativity and inventiveness and embrace our role as sophisticated professionals who are curious, persistent, savvy, and strategic. As proactive teachers, we will cleverly adapt good things from our current practice and take prudent risks as we invent new and better ways of engaging students in learning. We will use familiar practices in unfamiliar ways or convert existing practice to fit new goals as we redesign and renovate the American schoolhouse. As we metaphorically tear down walls to create new spaces and replace outdated wiring with sophisticated lighting systems, we will also look for new and effective uses for old hardwood flooring, structural beams, and glass doorknobs. We will experiment and invent in responsible ways. We will capitalize on our diverse experiences and skills and help one another overcome the fears that might hold us back.

The American teaching community is diverse. There are teachers who are dedicated to offering opportunities to underserved kids, who have dedicated their adult lives to impassioned teaching in high-expectations schools, who have contributed to the strong gains in reading and math performance in high-poverty areas all around the country. They have changed our understanding of equity, and their work is essential if education is to do what it should for individuals and society.

There are young educators, digital natives, who themselves benefited from (and perhaps made mistakes) using MOOCs and Facebook. They bring an understanding about becoming an adult professional in the twenty-first century that can and should inform all of us.

Others recognize all of this as a newer version of a belief they have always held—that teaching the whole child is the only way to build whole adults. They bring a deep understanding of the various kinds of learning and how to tap into the unique talents, interests, and experiences of each student.

Each of these teachers brings different capacities to the effort. Each of them may also feel different risks.

We need to understand and acknowledge the genuine risk many educators feel about redesigning our schools. If we let members of the broader community into our classrooms, they may respond with the same low level of understanding and high level of scrutiny we've experienced before. If we take on competencies beyond basic academic skills, we might lose sight of the unfinished and essential work of helping all kids develop academic skills. We may feel we know how to do school only one way and can't start over. We have to work together to overcome our fears, mitigate these risks, and learn to implement change.

Although they have access to the world's collective knowledge on their smart phones, today's children need guidance to learn how to make decisions about public and private information, how to distinguish quality information from gossip, and how to make decisions that are good for them and their neighbors. The current way we do school is not going to get them there.

The Mindset and Rationale for Intellectual Risk-Taking

2

What are you thinking right now?

For me, as a teacher, I have learned best and grown the most when someone asked me

- to think differently about something very specific

- provided me with a deep rationale for thinking differently

- invited me to argue with that rationale and find what I believed

- and then worked with me to find concrete ways to change my practice so it aligned with my newly refined beliefs.

In an effort to have that kind of interaction with you as we go on in this conversation, I'll periodically ask you to stop and take a moment to reflect, synthesize, or argue with what you've just read. The questions aren't commands but choices, so if you find yourself arguing with what you've just read or not wanting to answer them, that's important. Reflecting and determining your own clear purpose as a reader and teacher are essential components to being a responsible innovator. You will be the one to use your ideas, so trust your gut and use these prompts as much as is helpful to you.

Right now, I want to ask you to think about how closely your perspective aligns with the key beliefs asserted in Chapter 1.

What Do You Believe About Students?

The first two beliefs can be summarized by saying that in the twenty-first century, it is both necessary and possible to teach all students to be proactive learners, professionals, and community members. What's your thinking on each of these assertions?

Do you believe the twenty-first century has dramatically different demands and opportunities than the century before? Reflecting on this question should be pretty straightforward. Track a few thoughts below about whether you believe students need to grow up to be proactive learners, professionals, and community members to be successful twenty-first-century adults.

Do you believe all students can learn to be proactive adults equipped to be successful in this changed environment?

Let's slow down a little on the second question. Pull out a copy of your class list, and consider the first, fifth, ninth, and seventeenth students on the list. If you think about these individuals, which of the following descriptors would you attribute to each of them?

Proactive by Nature—These students already have a proactive disposition. They came to you this way, and they are a pleasure to teach.

Proactive by Hard Work—These students don't come by a proactive stance naturally, but they are hard-working, they have good models, and you can imagine them getting there by the time they graduate high school.

Not Made to Be Proactive—These students don't seem to engage or try. You see glimmers sometimes, but the pattern of their behavior seems to be that they are perpetually seeking the easy way out and can't be counted on to do things even when it is clear that it would be in their own self-interest to do so.

I don't know which kinds of students numbers one, five, nine, and seventeen are in your class, and maybe you have never met a kid that you thought wasn't made to be proactive. But I know that in my conversations with teachers, even teachers who feel a strong commitment to every child's ability to learn, there are sometimes kids they talk about as not made to be proactive. Too often when we talk about all kids being able to learn, we limit the scope of belief to academic content and skills. We think, "Any kid can learn to read, if he or she is willing to work hard," rather than, "What on earth can we do to teach that kid to work hard enough to become a fluent reader?"

When teachers take on the responsibility to teach all students to be proactive learners, professionals, and community members, they will certainly experience some failure. My hope is that educators use the responsible innovation process to get comfortable with small failures, maybe many of them, in an effort to resist quitting on those students who don't present as having it in their nature to be proactive. So I ask that as we innovate, we make a conscious effort to maintain the belief that all students can learn to be proactive.

What Do You Believe About Teachers?

Put together, the beliefs about teachers described in Chapter 1 basically come down to belief *in* teachers. Despite a culture of mistrust and a misunderstanding of the craft of teaching, I believe in the capacity of teachers not only to be creative problem solvers with their students but also to be able to help their neighbors come to trust their expertise.

I am so certain about the capacity of teachers that I suspect there are already many intentional things you do to teach your students to be proactive. I also suspect that some of those things are pretty inventive and creative. Take a moment to reflect on your normal routine, key projects, approaches to instruction, your teaching . . . and identify those things you already do to teach your students to be proactive learners, professionals, and community members.

There are also things you are doing to demonstrate your ability to be a proactive professional. What are the things you have done to inquire, investigate, collaborate, and evolve your teaching? Make note of those experiences here; they will enrich and support you as you go further into the responsible innovation process.

What Forces Feel Like They're Pushing Against Your Desire to Innovate?

You may have encountered a sense of mistrust from noneducators, policymakers, or district leaders. If so, what do you think are their fears, and as a result, what will help them feel good about redesigning school to promote the development of proactive learners, professionals, and community members?

Why might they be uncomfortable with widespread classroom innovation, and what might they need in order to see the value of innovation for the children in your community?

Keep these initial reflections in mind as you read about the responsible innovation process and ideas about converting and inventing practices in service of fostering proactive stances in your students.

Based on Your Beliefs, What Kind of Reader Will You Be?

If you are raring and ready to go, you might make a mental note now to remind yourself to be reasonable as you read—reasonable about what you try to take on, and how you imagine initial implementation will transform your classroom.

If you are finding yourself on the fence, you might try to sort ideas into categories.

- First steps. These are the ideas that align easily with your beliefs and build on your strengths. These are your entry points.

- Second steps. Ideas that intrigue you and that you may want to come back to after getting a few early wins from the first steps category.

- Third steps. These are the ideas that seem pretty far from either your current beliefs or what feel to you like reasonable next steps. Maybe the only action you take here is to find colleagues for whom these things were first steps and see if you can watch them try some of this.

And if you are finding yourself to be primarily resistant, that's OK. We can still have some great conversations, and I can't hear it when you raise your voice, so don't worry about offending me. Try to be deeply analytical as you read; try to discover exactly where you think the logic goes wrong. Consider asking yourself questions like:

- Do I disagree with the goal for students, or the way that we get there, or both?

- Do I think this is good to do but impossible because of factors around me?

- What do I think is more important than what is prioritized here, and why?

Use the answers to those questions to find a nugget of an idea that you can use to do something you aspire to do in your classroom.

Having established the premise for responsible innovation and gathering your initial thoughts, we are ready to hop into the process of responsible innovation.

Creating an Environment That Promotes Intellectual Risk-Taking

To engage in meaningful and shared innovation, it is essential that the culture among colleagues promote intellectual risk-taking. It is equally essential that classrooms have a culture that supports students in taking intellectual risks. Giving students opportunities to take intellectual risks and to fail are absolutely necessary to helping them learn to be proactive.

The fastest way to figure out how teachers either promote or prohibit intellectual risk-taking is to begin with reflection. When have you felt either very safe or very unsafe taking an intellectual risk? We can analyze those examples to determine the characteristics of safe learning environments.

I'll share a pair of related personal examples. Academic content disclaimer: These events took place in my third year of college. That was a *really* long time ago. If, in this example, I present ideas that you as an anthropology expert know to be false, please forgive me, as it is my best recollection.

In my third year of college, I was in a really interesting anthropology class. We explored complex concepts about evolution, human instinct, speed of human invention versus evolution, and other cool stuff. It was really interesting, and we regularly ran into questions that I had to think about really, really, really hard before I thought I was even beginning to get it. A professor who was best known for field research and publication taught this undergraduate class. When he wasn't in the field, I had the impression he was working with a small number of elite graduate students in active research courses. I also had the impression that he was forced to teach this class, and that he was certain it was a giant waste of both his talent and time. He projected an air of constant dissatisfaction and judgment. Rather unfortunately, his instructional style was to be an interactive lecturer. So he would routinely say things like, "We know this, this, this, and this—now what do you think that means?" And we would all sit quietly until he would sort of grunt in impatience and say, "It means this!"

You know how there are moments, small little moments, that sometimes go by and you wish you had had the courage to act differently? I have about a dozen or so of those moments that haunt me. Another time, we can discuss my third-grade fire prevention poster. But one of these dozen times happened in this anthropology class. The important, creative, and highly ranked professor was talking about how the biological process of adolescence and readying for adult life happen sooner in female humans than male humans. And I was following as he talked about how that is also true for other species, that maybe this related to the need to provide long-term care of offspring, that maybe this related to the roles males of the species played and females of the species played. And he asked, "Why would it be advantageous, and therefore favored in evolution of the species, for females to reach maturity sooner than their male counterparts?" And . . . I thought I knew the answer. If girls can have time to practice they can get good at both selecting and attracting high-quality mates, which ultimately gives their kids and their genes a better chance. I knew it. I was sure, and I sat there as silent as I had on any other day. Because the fear of being wrong and being savagely judged in front of my peers was so much greater than what I imagined would be the accolades if I were correct. So, I held my breath until I heard the inevitable grunt and him saying, "It is because they can practice." Then he went on to explain the same thinking I had just done in my head.

On that day, and future days in that class, I sat silent even when I was really sure I had done some good thinking. Sharing was too risky. However, that class also had a weekly discussion group. My group had about a dozen students. When we met, we didn't meet with the important professor; instead, we met with an unimportant but really great TA.

With our TA, we looked at multiple examples of a concept or phenomenon. She asked us what patterns we saw across these examples. Then she asked us to theorize about the *many* reasons why that pattern might be happening, and how that related to whatever question we were grappling with. We shared all kinds of crazy ideas. She told us when our ideas were nuts or interesting. She fed us other examples and asked us other smaller questions, like breadcrumbs to follow.

One day the question was, why does evolution have less impact on things that happen later in the lifespan of humans? In other words, if many of the physical changes associated with aging were crummy, and there were some people who seemed to suffer fewer of these common ailments (existing genetic potential), why hadn't evolution taken care of it? She showed us a bunch of graphs illustrating of the numbers of people living in different age groups in many different human populations all around the world and in different periods of time. The graph below is an approximation from my mental note, which is now well over twenty years old, so please don't hold me to the specifics in this graph, but I believe the common shape of the many graphs was similar to Figure 2.1.

For all kinds of human populations, in all kinds of places, in different periods in time— the shape of the data was something like this. My immediate response was, it is good to be a woman. But my second thought was, why was that true? I, and others, asked our TA a lot of questions about why the data looked like this. She pointed out that the gap

Figure 2.1 Populations by Age, Geography, and Time Period

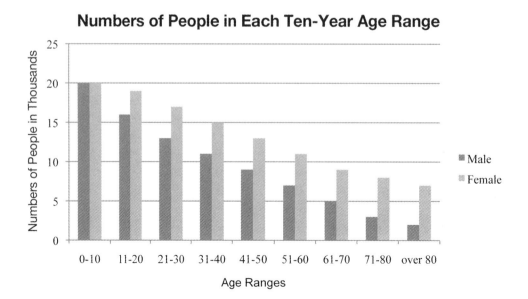

between males and females was mostly created in early adulthood and then each group continued to shrink at relatively similar rates. Then she asked us what was something we knew about male behavior in that time historically. We talked about early adulthood being a time when males are engaged in a lot of dangerous behavior: wars, protecting their family, demonstrating manliness for the benefit of possible mates, and so on.

Then we got back to the general shape of the data. Why were there fewer people over time? We ended up deciding that just by chance, accidents, wars, bad crops, and disease, that a lot of humans are gone before we hit advanced age. Then she asked, what does that have to do with evolution not favoring those people who "age well."

It was a moment just like in lecture. I knew it, and in this environment, I didn't hesitate. I said, "Because there aren't enough people left in that phase of the lifecycle to really influence the gene pool, and, for most of us (women), things about our physical characteristics that make us more or less likely to mate successfully have all played out before we get to the point where nature has exposed whether we will age well or not." My TA said that yes, I was on the right track, and then went on to offer some technical language and clarification to my response and then went on asking us more questions.

I remember this moment with the same clarity and emotional intensity as the moment when I was too afraid to speak. I felt smart and courageous. I felt valued. I had contributed to our collective understanding of really difficult stuff, and my community appreciated it. I was hooked; I wanted to keep trying to understand, trying to share, and trying to participate in our group's learning.

What Are You Thinking Now?

When have you been made hesitant or brave by the environment you were in?

What were the characteristics in each environment that most contributed to your fear or courage?

_____

_____

I don't know for sure, but I suspect there are some commonalities to the characteristics that have made us fearful or brave. How can we make our staff rooms and classrooms places where adults and children feel supported in being courageous? Based on this reflection and observations in hundreds of classrooms since, I have come to believe that to promote intellectual risk-taking, classroom environments need to be characterized like this . . .

- There is a persistent expectation that the group, and each member of the group, will figure it out.

- Learners are supported in their inquiry. Teachers leave them breadcrumbs and give new breadcrumbs when students ask questions or get stuck.

- There is a persistent valuing of all ideas (even the really crazy ones) that are serious attempts to make sense of things.

- There is consistent, honest feedback about which ideas have more or less merit, and the logic used to assess that merit is transparent to everyone.

- There is time to think and work on your own.

- There is time to think and work with a few others.

- There is time to think and try out ideas as a whole group.

- The group has a way to notice or mark the occasion when great thinking happens.

Reflect on those things that define the culture among colleagues in your school. How do you speak to and about one another? Do normal ways of communicating support a shared belief in your individual and collective ability to figure it out? How does the group respond to crazy ideas? Is your culture one where it is OK to be really awesome at something, and where it is also OK to be open about what you aren't great at?

Reflect on those things that define the culture in your classroom. How do you speak to and about students? Does it send a message of your persistent expectation that they will figure it out? How do you respond to crazy ideas? How can you tell the difference between crazy distracting ideas and ones that are serious, if failed, attempts to make sense of things? How often do you resist the urge to demonstrate that you are the smartest one in the room, that you have the answer, and instead lay a new trail of breadcrumbs to lead your students to find the answer on their own?

As you reflect on your practice in this way, is there one thing you want to do differently to contribute to a shift in the culture among adults in your school? Or one thing you want to do differently to make your classroom a place that gives students the courage to participate?

If so—write those one or two things down here. Make that secret commitment to yourself to try doing something a little differently.

What Is a Responsible Innovation Process?

The Fallacy of "Scientifically Proven" Practices in Education

In everyday conversation I think it is really fun to throw around inflammatory language, like "fallacy." However, in writing things down to share with new colleagues in this book, I agonized for many hours over whether to use that word here. So let me be super, extra clear about what idea I am trying to be inflammatory about. I do not think that scientific research is falsely scientific or lacks validity—rather I think that the practice of relying on scientific research to ensure quality work in schools is accidentally impeding quality.

The attention to scientifically based research as a measure of value in education has come from a place of very good intentions. We want to do the very best things with our children. We don't want to experiment and be irresponsible or at all disrespectful of the gift of time we have been given with children in our K–12 system.

There is also a smart political value driving these practices. The people responsible for doling out public money don't want to say to their constituents that they are investing in experimentation. They want to say they are investing in scientifically proven methods. They want to know that there is no risk associated with their investment, because they are responsible for making the best use of public funds.

Both of these perspectives, from a distance, are entirely reasonable. So reasonable that if a person didn't dig more deeply, it might seem ridiculous to challenge the practice of requiring scientifically proven methods in education.

Digging a bit deeper to see the result of this way of doing things, however, we see that it has made education more stagnant and less able to learn and adapt than nearly any other industry. Here is how this process generally plays out.

Step 1: Smart people working in some school in America have a good new idea. They try it in their room or school, and they see some compelling results. This process takes three to five years because results are compelling only if they include a few years of standardized testing data.

Step 2: Someone from a university comes to scientifically study what they have done, and then they publish the findings. This takes another one to two years.

Step 3: A publishing company develops a packaged set of tools or resources to do what the smart people thought up seven years ago, and they use the research that was completed to justify the effectiveness of their product. This takes a year.

Step 4: Schools can buy that product and be trained in how to use it to try what the smart people tried. These teachers pilot it with 100 percent fidelity for two to three years.

Step 5: After analyzing the results of the pilot, the school either ditches the product for something else or decides that it needs to be adapted for use with their students.

Step 6a: The school spends special paid extra time in the summer to make the adaptations and then train their team on how to implement the adapted approach with fidelity.

OR

Step 6b: The school will spend special paid extra time in the summer to review new products and ideas to determine what to try next.

I realize I have rounded all timeframes to full years, but even if I am off by two or three years, this is an intolerably inefficient way to develop, share, and promote quality work.

Placing this process back in the context of the pace of change in the twenty-first century:

- What else was happening as the ten years of this process unfolded?

- What new technology emerged?

- What societal shifts occurred?

- How has the job market changed?

- How do we know whether this idea, the new good idea of ten years ago, is still a good idea today?

Let's Fail Faster and Learn Faster

Individually and collectively, we can learn faster. And, we still need to learn in a way that is mindful of our commitment to do the very best we can with the kids in our community. Being mindful of this commitment means vetting ideas well and ensuring faster failure and faster learning. For the good of our students and the use of public funds, we need to ensure that we don't need a full three years of implementation to determine that something isn't working. We can manage the risk of trying new things by trying new ideas in a short, time-bound way and using clear leading indicators to evaluate impact.[1]

Using an agreed-upon process helps mitigate and manage the risk of allowing ourselves to innovate. A process helps our community trust that we aren't wasting students' time or public money, but that on the contrary, we are working in smart, efficient, and analytical ways to drive fast improvement. I'm about to go into detail explaining a responsible process for innovation, but first, here's two visuals of what that can look like (see Figures 3.1 and 3.2).

Figure 3.1 Innovation Process for Educators

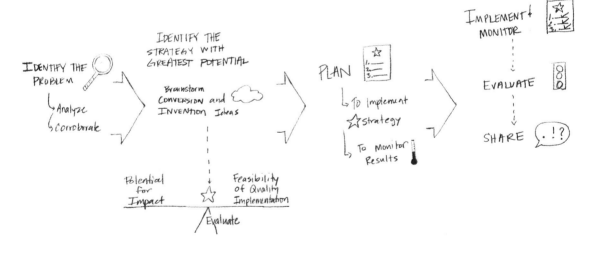

[1] While I created this specific process to emphasize both speed and quality, it should be noted that my design was informed by the work of others who have created other processes for teacher action research. I would specifically like to thank the good people at 2 Revolutions (check them out at 2revolutions.net) and my good friend and colleague Dana Frazee for our recent conversations about how to help teachers fail, succeed, and learn faster.

Figure 3.2 Phase, Time, and Tasks of Education Innovation

Phase of the Work	Estimated Timeframe	Tasks
Identification	2–4 hours	• Identify the thing you want to make better (the problem). • Identify the idea (strategy) with maximum potential to solve the problem.
Planning	8–12 hours	• Articulate the rationale that supports that idea. • Determine what results implementing that idea should yield in the very short term. • Determine how to gather information about those results. • Map out implementation steps, and build whatever tools you need to try it out.
Implementation and Monitoring	Between 2 and 10 weeks	• Try it. • Gather information and monitor results.
Analysis	2 hours	• Evaluate results with colleagues.
Impact	Timing depends on result	Based on results do one of these three things: 1. If results are bad, analyze the work and rationale to understand why it failed, and never do it or other things with those bad premises again. Share that learning with your colleagues to prevent them from the same failure. 2. If the results are mixed, analyze to understand what worked and didn't. Revisit rationale to see if it still holds up. Try to fix it and repeat the process. 3. If the results were positive, figure out how to share it with your colleagues so they can benefit from your smart ideas and good work.

It's Not Just the Process: Mindset Also Matters

Processes can be a great help, but they rarely yield the intended result if we just follow them blindly. Our understanding of the rationale and our mindset inform whether we implement a process proactively and whether we get the results we need. Review and evaluate this summary of the rationale behind the responsible innovation process.

Figure 3.3 The Rationale for Responsible Innovation

Statements That Define the Rationale for Responsible Innovation	Do you agree?		
	Yes!	Kind of.	No.
Teachers are bright, creative, and dedicated professionals who are great at learning new things and skilled at noticing patterns in how individual students respond to subtle changes in their instruction.			
Collaboration among smart colleagues with diverse experiences results in better ideas.			
Innovation or invention does not, by itself, satisfy any important purpose. Innovation or invention are really worthy only if they result in making something better.			
There is only so much we can know about how something will work before we actually try it and a significant diminishing return on investing time in trying to imagine what will take an idea from great to perfection before we give it a try.			
There are always things we can either observe or inquire about with students that will tell us whether we are on the right track or not.			
The only way for groups of colleagues to learn quickly, and not repeat the same inquiries, is to be open about both failure and success.			

If you disagree with components of the rationale, you may find that some components of the process feel less valuable than others. If you choose to adapt the process to better fit your beliefs, please do strive to maintain commitment to both fast and responsible learning.

It is important to both understand and monitor mindset. It's easy to begin a day or a school year with a sense of possibility and end it with a sense of disappointment. It is easy to let small failures or frustrations affect mindset, making it even more difficult to do what we set out to do. It is helpful to have mindset shorthand that can be frequently revisited to determine when and how to adjust mindset to maximize the chance of things working as originally planned. I encourage you to revisit the following "Rules of Play" as you plan, implement, and analyze impact. Staying in the right frame of mind makes it easier to learn and increases the chances of success.

Rules of Play for an Innovation Mindset

1. Learning Trumps Ego:

Being humble, open, and honest with ourselves and colleagues is an essential component to learning as a community. It also helps us learn faster.

Learning trumping ego in this process looks like:
- When bouncing ideas around with colleagues, listen carefully and be open to their questions, critiques, and suggestions. Be open to the idea that there may be something you haven't thought of yet, and use your colleagues to help you identify any missing pieces.
- When you are implementing, ask others to come in and watch. It may be messy, but the purpose of them watching isn't to judge you as a teacher; it is to analyze the effects of your strategy and help you learn.
- When you get to the end and you think you are onto something, present it to your colleagues with openness to new questions and critique. To seriously consider taking your ideas and doing something with it, strong colleagues will need to question your thinking and wonder about how it might work in their room. The most powerful recognition any of us can receive for our good work is a colleague's willingness to take that learning into their room.
- If you get to the end and you discover that your effort was primarily a failure, share that with confidence. Be confident in your relationships with your colleagues and the quality of your practice. Engage your colleagues in helping you figure out why it didn't work. This learning will benefit everyone and may result in new better ideas to try.

2. Don't Let Great Be the Enemy of Good:

When we are willing to trust our expertise and try implementing things when they are really good, maybe 80 percent of the way there, rather than waiting to make them perfect, we end up finding perfect faster. When we try to figure out the remaining 20 percent by running through multiple scenarios in our minds, or creating a dozen different permutations of our idea, we may feel more certain but are still very unlikely to have it 100 percent right.

Not letting great be the enemy of good in this process looks like:
- When you and your colleagues think an idea is 80 percent right, you start trying it out. You try it out because you trust your collective expertise and believe that the vast majority of the time, if you all agree that an idea is a good idea, you will be right.
- As you implement, you and your colleagues monitor leading indicators closely and try to correlate changes in those indicators with changes in delivery, tools, or strategies.
- As you and your colleagues learn from that monitoring, you make adjustments to strategy.
- You and your colleagues repeat that process until you reach the end of your trial period, at which point, you do an in-depth analysis of the impact of your strategy on your problem.

3. Be Measured:

Be disciplined about how much you take on and disciplined in how carefully you implement the Responsible Innovation Process.

Being measured while implementing this process looks like . . .
- From the beginning, you and your colleagues resist the urge to take on a change so complex and multidimensional that it isn't possible to identify why it works or doesn't work. You choose something discrete and focused.
- In your excitement to get going, you and your colleagues resist the urge to start without clearly identifying the indicators you will use to measure impact. You also plan for how you will collect and analyze that information throughout the period of initial implementation. Innovation without measures undermines the trust we need to build with our communities.
- You and your colleagues hold yourselves accountable to the timeline you originally set out. You stop when you said you would stop, thoroughly evaluate progress, and decide whether to: stop it, fix it, or share it. Being disciplined in this process supports fast learning.

What Are You Thinking Now?

What does adopting this mindset do for someone in terms of helping them participate in the process of redesign or invention in a positive and safe way?

_____

_____

If someone were to participate without one or more of the components of this mindset, how might they feel as they engage in the process?

_____

_____

What could a person do to be a leader in working with his or her colleagues in this way? How could someone help build a "community of doers" willing to work in this deeply collaborative, honest, and analytical way?

_____

_____

How does modeling these mindsets or dispositions connect back to being a proactive learner, professional, and community member?

_____

_____

Can't resist . . . I know this is probably two reflection questions too many . . . but I have one more: Does this spark any ideas about how to help your students develop as proactive learners, professionals, and community members? You were probably already having ideas about this anyway . . . I am just giving you space to capture those ideas.

Identify the Problem and Problem-Solving Strategy

Phase, Time, and Tasks of Education Innovation

Phase of the Work	Estimated Timeframe	Tasks
Identification	2–4 hours	• Identify the thing you want to make better (the problem). • Identify the idea (strategy) with maximum potential to solve the problem.

Excerpt from main table on page 35

Identification, Step One: Identify the Problem

What do you want to make better (what's the problem)?

This is a frequently underrated portion of innovation processes. While one of the two stated priorities of this process is to speed things up, it is worth slowing down just a little bit here to be sure you have your work aimed at the right target. Slowing down a bit helps minimize the risk that the significant effort of trying to convert or invent is misspent fixing the wrong problem.

It helps to

- start by identifying and framing the problem so that it sits squarely within your sphere of control

- take the time to ask why that problem is happening and why that underlying cause is happening, and so on, a few times

- look for correlations in data or seek expertise to corroborate your analysis.

Identify and Situate the Problem Within Your Sphere of Control

Trying to solve problems that are beyond our control is a waste of time.

So if the first problem that comes to mind is something like, "I have more English language learners than I'm used to," we aren't really empowered to change that problem. If we begin to ask why that is true, we don't uncover important things we could be doing differently. That is not to say that things beyond our control aren't having a dramatic impact on our classrooms. They impact teachers and students in powerful ways, but rather than fret about or be mad about those things, we make more progress when we spend our energy trying to impact the parts we can change. We are more empowered when we identify problems like: "The strategies I have for supporting English language learners aren't working now that I have more than one or two English language learners in my class," or, "My students don't know how to collaborate effectively," or, "My students don't have chances to fail—and learn from failure—at school."

Sometimes it helps to acknowledge that there's stuff outside of our control (see Figure 4.1). We have to get that out of the way—clear the pipes—for the stuff we can control. So give yourself space to do that here.

Figure 4.1 Moving from What I Can't to What I Can Control (Example: ELLs)

Problem	Is that problem within or outside my control?	If outside, what I am struggling to do related to this problem?	How could I frame the issue within my locus of control?
I have many more English language learners than I am used to.	Not really inside—I can't control the changing demographics at my school.	I don't feel like I am effectively teaching ELL students academic content knowledge.	I need to develop specific strategies for helping new English speakers learn both the content and vocabulary of academic content.

Problem	Is that problem within or outside my control?	If outside, what am I struggling to do related to this problem?	How could I frame the issue within my locus of control?

Why Is That Problem Happening?

Despite the fact that this behavior of repeatedly asking "why" is most commonly associated with charming preschoolers, it can be used to identify important and less obvious underlying causes for problems. It is important to take a bit of time trying to identify why the problem is happening, so we can aim our efforts at the deepest underlying cause within our sphere of control.

Throughout exploration of this process, we will build an example using the problem, "My students don't know how to collaborate."

We begin work on that problem by asking, why, why, why? If I were talking to myself about this problem, the analysis might go something like you see in Figure 4.2.

This is a much narrower and more specific problem to tackle than, "My students don't know how to collaborate." And that problem leads to two narrow strategies that I could try with students. I could take steps to make the rationale for collaboration clear to my students and model at least one approach to collaborative work with that rationale in mind.

The essential takeaway is that problem solving is a complex process in which our first question should lead to more questions. So, while filling out a form like this may offer an oversimplified view of the thinking required, try to use the simplicity of the prompts to support persistence in the analysis. We need to keep asking "why" to find the core cause of the problem.

Figure 4.2 One Way to Work Through Problem Identification (Example: Collaboration)

The first question is . . .	The answer might be . . .
Why don't kids know how to collaborate?	~~They spend all their time in inauthentic interactions with people online, and they don't know how to relate to real people.~~ Out of locus of control, try again . . . I haven't invested the time to teach them to do it well.
The second question might be . . .	**The answer might be . . .**
Why haven't I taught them how to do it well?	Because, in my language arts curriculum, they described small-group work and collaboration as a strategy to make skill practice more engaging. But because my students are so bad at collaborating, it doesn't actually engage them in practice or learning. It just engages them with one another.
The third question might be . . .	**The answer might be . . .**
Why do adults usually collaborate—is it to make their work more engaging?	Maybe, it is fun to work together. But I think as an adult, collaboration is most meaningful to me not because of the company but because other people have different and sometimes better ideas than I do.
The fourth question might be . . .	**The answer might be . . .**
Why don't my students see that as the purpose of collaboration?	I never asked them to. I thought the work of practicing skills together would be more fun than doing it on your own. Maybe I was asking them to collaborate about the wrong things. Maybe collaboration is a better match for problem solving.

So, the most basic problem here is

that I wasn't clear about the purpose of collaboration, and as a result, I didn't share either a clear rationale for collaborating or a model of a way to collaborate that helps one another think.

Try analyzing a problem from your classroom here. I'm going to ask you to use this problem to practice each step of the process as you continue to read.

The first question is . . .	The answer might be . . .
The second question might be . . .	The answer might be . . .
The third question might be . . .	The answer might be . . .
The fourth question might be . . .	The answer might be . . .

So, the most basic problem here is

Corroborate or Debunk with Data and/or Expertise

As I continue to pursue the problem above, there are a number of good questions and directions I could pursue to corroborate or debunk my idea about the core problem.

The easiest way to get corroborated, or be debunked, is to ask an expert colleague. If I could find someone in my school or district with expertise, I could ask him or her if he or she thinks collaboration is a better match for problem-solving tasks than it has been for skill practice. If my expert colleague thinks that matching the strategy of collaboration with the right kind of task isn't a big reason students struggle with collaboration, he or she could give me a different idea about where to focus first. Maybe my colleague is willing to come in and observe my students collaborating in skill practice and help me identify other possible root causes that I missed.

Another good way to corroborate or debunk my identification of the problem is to see if there are any data or other information I could correlate with my identification of the problem. For example, I could ask my teammates whether they have had much success using collaboration as a way to make practice engaging, or whether they have had much success using collaboration to support problem solving. Their responses would help me know whether I was on the right track.

For other problems there may be other information or data that could be used. If, distinct from this example regarding collaboration, my team identified a small group of students having a hard time in their math class, but who were still right on track in all of their other academic classes—we might look to see when they have math class. If math is first period, or in the period immediately after lunch, we might look to attendance data to see if the underlying issue impacting their math performance is that they are chronically arriving late to first period or chronically returning late from our open-campus lunch.

Corroborating thinking is part of how we make innovation responsible. While we don't want innovation to happen outside our room or school and be given to us to implement with fidelity, we aren't doing all we can to get great quickly if we don't take advantage of the expertise of others. None of us knows it all. Responsible innovators use the writing, practice, and experience of others to find the underlying problem with greater speed and accuracy.

Identification, Step Two: Identify Which Strategy You Should Start With

Once the problem is identified, generating strategies can be pretty straightforward. For some problems, one good conversation with colleagues is enough to generate a wide range of strategies to consider. If the problem is one that is less familiar to colleagues, it might make sense to do some reading to learn what colleagues in other places have tried. Whatever resource makes sense for the teacher and the focus of the responsible innovation process, this is the time to get some help identifying and vetting strategies.

This is also the time to decide whether to convert an existing practice so it has new potential to address your problem or whether this is a situation for invention. It is most prudent to think in practical terms when deciding whether to convert or invent practices to help students develop proactive capacity.

Sometimes a new idea, one that is untested, will appear to be the simplest and most direct way to make the change you wish to see in your classroom. When that is the case, go with invention. When you are ready to invent, go to Chapter 8, starting on page 98, to learn about how to engage with colleagues to think from scratch and invent something new.

And at other times, there will be something you or a colleague is doing that does a lot to help students develop one capacity or another, and it is easy to imagine that one or two changes to that practice would support students in developing one or more proactive capacities without compromising the existing value. When you have your eye on conversion, go to Chapter 7, starting on page 74, to explore how instructional protocols, assessment for learning practices, and daily routines can be converted and put to new use.

The point here is that confidence in the potential of the idea, rather than choosing to be forever on "team invention" or "team conversion," is the most effective approach.

Once there is a list of possible strategies, perhaps a combination of converted and invented ideas, it is time to place bets and decide which one to implement first. In some cases, this can be a pretty quick process. If there are two or three ideas competing for best idea, and each of them is aimed squarely at a problem that has been identified and corroborated—you may not need a lot of science to determine which to try first.

If there is a strategy that naturally rises to the top, name that strategy and move on.

If what to try first isn't readily apparent, list a few strategy ideas in the template on page 50. Then use the questions provided to help compare strategies and determine which strategy to begin. Figure 4.3 and the following narrative (using the continuing example of my students' learning to collaborate) illustrate the kind of thinking I would do when considering which strategy to try.

This is an important point in the process to remember to be measured and resist the temptation to take on too much. But that doesn't mean that some combining or pairing of strategies is bad. In evaluating the brainstormed ideas in our continuing example, I

Figure 4.3 Consideration of Strategies (Example: Collaboration)

	Questions to Consider
Strategy 1: Build a collaboration boot camp, where we practice specific collaboration skills with not very new content, then practice with complex tasks.	• Which option is easiest for you to try? • Which option has the fewest, or easiest to mitigate, possible negative risks associated with it? • Which option do your colleagues think has the greatest potential?
Strategy 2: Train up a set of super collaborators so they can model strong collaboration for others in my class.	• Which option do your colleagues think they would also like to try? • Which option requires the fewest resources to deliver with quality?
Strategy 3: Jump right into trying to collaborate on a rigorous problem-solving task so students see the value and also the difference.	• Would one of the options inherently produce data that would help you evaluate effectiveness? • Does one of these options align more closely to the shared values and mission of your school?
Strategy 4: Write up a few examples or narratives that describe situations in which people might work together, and ask students to identify whether they would or would not want to collaborate in those situations and why—then use that information to generate shared definitions of working together to complete separate tasks versus collaborating to make sense of something or do something difficult.	• Which option does your well-informed gut say will have the greatest impact?

might select pairing strategies 2 and 3. I would choose those two ideas because I think that getting them to see the value of collaborating in problem-solving situations is important, but without some modeling and support is too risky. By pairing the ideas I feel like I am maximizing potential and minimizing risk.

This is also an important time to remember not to let great be the enemy of good. It is important to keep in mind at this step in the process. If you are 80 percent sure it is the highest potential strategy in terms of addressing the problem and something you can pull off with quality—try it. Trying it sooner, while using the responsible innovation process, will make things better faster for your students. So, don't agonize too much here. If your idea aligns with the problem, and you are sure of the problem—there is a very good chance it will have a positive impact on students.

Use this template to capture potential strategies to address the problem you identified on page 46, and use the "Questions to Consider" to hone in on the strategy you wish to try first.

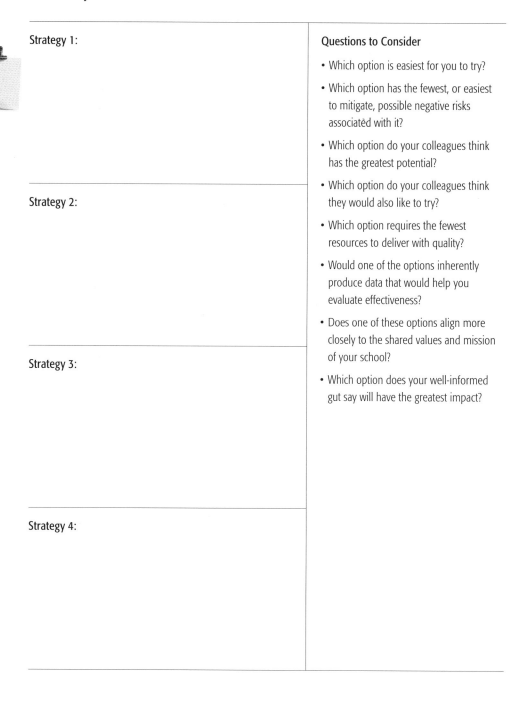

Strategy 1:

Strategy 2:

Strategy 3:

Strategy 4:

Questions to Consider

- Which option is easiest for you to try?

- Which option has the fewest, or easiest to mitigate, possible negative risks associated with it?

- Which option do your colleagues think has the greatest potential?

- Which option do your colleagues think they would also like to try?

- Which option requires the fewest resources to deliver with quality?

- Would one of the options inherently produce data that would help you evaluate effectiveness?

- Does one of these options align more closely to the shared values and mission of your school?

- Which option does your well-informed gut say will have the greatest impact?

Plan

Phase, Time, and Tasks of Education Innovation

Phase of the Work	Estimated Timeframe	Tasks
Planning	8–12 hours	• Articulate the rationale that supports that idea. • Determine what results implementing that idea should yield in the very short term. • Determine how to gather information about those results. • Map out implementation steps, and build whatever tools you need to try it out.

Excerpt from main table on page 35

Rationale: Why Are You Going to Try This Strategy?

This is the part of innovation planning that is distinct from other planning processes. It is important to have a clear and concise written rationale for what you plan to try. Taking the time to write it down now will help you synthesize why you are trying something different; it will also help you more easily explain to your students, families, and colleagues what you are trying and why. The written rationale will also help you evaluate this work later. This should be something you can do quickly, as you have deeply explored the rationale when you identified the problem and the strategy you hope will address it.

For our running example regarding teaching students to collaborate, the rationale might look like Figure 5.1.

Figure 5.1 Sample Rationale (Example: Collaboration)

Rationale

The problem I originally brought into this process was that my students don't know how to collaborate. After thinking through potential causes on my own and talking with my colleagues, I have determined that I wasn't clear about the purpose of collaboration and kind of confused dividing up work tasks with collaborating. As a result, I didn't share either a clear vision or rationale for collaborating, or a model of a way to collaborate that helps one another think.

I selected two strategies, first to engage my students in problem-solving tasks that really require collaboration. I think this is essential because trying to be collaborative on tasks that I could do on my own is frustrating and I think my students may be experiencing the same thing. But I also think this is risky, because my students haven't had any practice with real collaboration. So, I decided to pair the strategy of giving students rigorous problem-solving tasks with the strategy about training up a small group of students so they can model for the rest of the group how to be good collaborators who listen, ask good questions, assert new ideas, and keep their group moving.

I think that by pairing these two strategies I will do the bold thing required to really help my students learn about collaboration, but I will avoid wasting time in unproductive or overly painful attempts. I don't think having a model will prevent all failure or frustration, but I think it will reduce it.

Now, take a moment and use the space below to identify your rationale for the strategy you identified on page 50.

Rationale

What Data Should I Be Gathering and How Should I Gather It?

As you imagine beginning to implement your strategy, what do you think you will be able to see in the first few weeks to help you determine whether this strategy is working or not? One of the promises of using the responsible innovation process is that failure will be spotted and addressed quickly. Before implementing, it is essential to determine how you will know quickly if the strategy is working.

The content of the strategy will impact which kinds of observations will be most helpful in evaluating the effectiveness of the strategy. I suggest considering three categories of quick results: observable behaviors of students, things students may say if the strategy is working, and changes in students' work. In Figure 5.2, there are examples of the kinds of early results I anticipate seeing in the continuing example regarding student collaboration.

Figure 5.2 Data Collection (Example: Collaboration)

	What to look for . . .
Observable student behaviors	I might observe students • trying to take turns instead of talking over one another • posing questions to their group • asking individuals specific questions • looking at one another's work • nodding their heads in agreement with their peers, or shaking their heads in disagreement • repeating good ideas they heard from their peers.
What students may say if the strategy is working	My students may say things like . . . • What do you think we should do next? • I don't get it. Can you explain that to me? • I disagree, and this is why . . . When asked about collaboration, my students may say things like . . . • Collaboration is difficult. • Collaboration helps us figure things out. • Collaboration isn't just giving out jobs.

continues

	What to look for . . .
Changes that can be observed by examining student work	In individual work products created during and after collaborative time . . . • Students will include ideas in their individual work that originated from another member of the group. • More students will be able to produce individual work that demonstrates understanding. In work products created by the group . . . • Each student will be able to point to ideas they contributed. • Each student will be able to point to ideas that came from others.

As you continue to practice the process, what information could you collect to evaluate the effectiveness of the strategy you identified on page 50?

	What to look for . . .
Observable student behaviors	
What students may say if the strategy is working	
Changes that can be observed by examining student work	

Sometimes tools or plans with colleagues will be necessary to actually collect the information needed to evaluate whether the strategy is working. Before digging into detailed planning or implementation, take a moment to identify what work may need to be done to collect the required information (see Figure 5.3).

Figure 5.3 How Will You Gather Data?

- Do you need to create an observation tool?
- Will you be able to observe for these things yourself, or do you need help from colleagues?
- Could you create a student reflection tool? How frequently do you want to ask them to notice whether the strategy is helping them in the way you intended?
- Could you create a pre and post student survey?
- What opportunities are coming to see impact on in-class assessments or participation in interim assessments?
- What kinds of changes do you think you will see first? What kinds of changes do you not expect to see right away, but you do expect to see later in the timeframe in which you plan to implement?

For the continuing example of student collaboration, I identified the following plans for collecting information (see Figure 5.4).

Figure 5.4 Plans for Collecting Information (Example: Collaboration)

	What to look for . . .	How to collect that information
Observable student behaviors	I might observe students • Trying to take turns instead of talking over one another • Posing questions to their group • Asking individuals specific questions • Looking at one another's work • Nodding their heads in agreement with their peers, or shaking their heads in disagreement • Repeating good ideas they heard from their peers	I can best collect observation data for each of these in the following way: • I really need to create a clean and easy-to-use observation tool. If I can identify exactly what about collaboration our experts will model and will label in that model I can then put those same things into the observation tool. The list to the left is probably about right, but I should think about it again before training the experts, etc. • I would like to plan to use the tool myself and ask my principal to observe using the tool. Maybe my colleague too, if she can get freed up to come in while I am teaching this.

continues

	What to look for . . .	How to collect that information
What students may say if the strategy is working	My students may say things like . . . • What do you think we should do next? • I don't get it. Can you explain that to me? • I disagree, and this is why . . . When asked about collaboration, my students may say things like . . . • Collaboration is difficult. • Collaboration helps us figure things out. • Collaboration isn't just giving out jobs.	I can best collect their perceptions by . . . • A lot of this can also be built into the observation tool. • However, I think I would like to ask my students in a warm-up before we begin all of this to define collaboration. Then after a week or so of doing this work, give an exit ticket where I either ask them what collaboration is . . . or use the stem, "I used to think . . . and now think . . ."
Changes that can be observed by examining student work	In individual work products created during and after collaborative time . . . • Students will include ideas in their individual work that originated from another member of the group. • More students will be able to produce individual work that demonstrates understanding. In work products created by the group . . . • Each student will be able to point to ideas they contributed. • Each student will be able to point to ideas that came from others.	I can gather and analyze that data by . . . These are a little tricky, unless I ask students to label ideas that came from them. I am not sure I can do this reliably. Also—I don't think I want to ask students to stick Post-it® notes with their names on them next to their ideas in a group work product. I don't want to promote the idea that being a good collaborator means getting the most ideas into the team's work. So, if I want to use those measures, I will need to do it in conversation. However—I can track whether collaboration is resulting in more students being able to demonstrate understanding in their individual work. Generally, in the first assessment of new problem-solving work about 60 percent of students get it. I can compare the percentage getting it in the first individual work to that bar.

These steps, determining observable results and planning to collect the necessary information to evaluate those results, aren't always intuitive. So let's slow down a little here and, in addition to continuing with the example regarding collaboration, let's dig into a second detailed example.

A few years ago, I was working with a K–8 school as they studied and implemented assessment for learning strategies (for a full explanation of how to maximize the use of assessment for learning practices, see page 85). In our professional development plans, we always identified the following:

- the long-term learning target for staff

- the smaller supporting targets that staff would work toward on their way to the long-term target

- a description of what making progress toward the targets may look like in terms of teacher actions

- a description of how we anticipated students would respond if teachers made progress toward learning targets.

Figure 5.5 shows what one section of the professional development plan looked like. As you read, see if you can spot the logical connections built from the long-term target all the way down to anticipated student results.

Figure 5.5 Plan for Assessment (Example: PD on Collaboration)

Teacher Long-Term Learning Target

I can use my deep knowledge about my students and assessment <u>for</u> learning practices to match instruction to my students' needs.

Supporting Targets

- I can weave both long-term and supporting-learning targets into my lesson design.
- I can narrow the focus of my instruction to the learning targets being addressed.
- I can provide students with clear descriptive feedback orally and in writing.
- I can narrow the focus of my descriptive feedback to the learning targets being addressed.
- I can design learning targets to emphasize areas that my students need.

Teacher Actions May Include:

- Teacher identifying the long-term target(s) the work that day is in service of
- Teacher identifying the supporting target(s) students will work toward today or for the next few days as a means of reaching the long-term target

---

continues

- Teacher sharing the supporting target(s) with students at the beginning of the lesson to help students know what they should be learning by working through the activities of the lesson
- Teacher sharing the long-term target(s) or guiding question to help students feel reason to make progress toward the supporting target(s)
- Teacher using the minilesson as a way to explicitly teach to the supporting-learning targets (modeling, group analysis, think-aloud, etc.)
- Teacher staying focused on the supporting-learning targets when conferring or pulling individuals or small groups for additional instruction
- Teacher staying focused on supporting-learning targets when collecting observation-based assessment data during the work/practice time
- In debrief, teacher asks that students reflect on what progress they made toward the supporting target
- Sometimes in debrief, teacher also asks students to reflect on how today's learning is helping them make progress toward the long-term target or guiding question

Anticipated Student Outcomes

- Students feel a need (reason) to learn the content of instruction.
- Students feel that instruction meets their needs and/or comes just when they need it.
- Students can describe their progress.
- Students advocate for themselves and seek help.
- Students feel good about the progress they have made individually and as a group, in the short term and long term.

We created this plan by continuing to ask ourselves, "What would it be like if?"

What would it look like if teachers were successful at narrowing the focus of my descriptive feedback to the learning targets being addressed?

It might mean that teachers stay focused on the supporting-learning targets when conferring or pulling individuals or small groups for additional instruction, and similarly, that teachers stay focused on supporting-learning targets when collecting observation-based assessment data during the work/practice time.

How would students feel and what would they think if teachers successfully stayed focused on supporting-learning targets when they conferred with them and provided instruction?

It might mean that students would feel that instruction meets their needs or that instruction comes just when they need it.

What Students Say When It's Working

While working closely with Liza Eaton, a middle school science teacher, I agreed to interview her students to find out if her implementation was yielding the anticipated result. So in this situation, my interview was one of the planned data-collection methods. What follows is a subset of the student responses.

How are you using the learning targets?

"I like that we talk about it (the targets) at the beginning of class. And then if we don't learn something we notice that."

"I think the target helps you know what to look for and what you need to focus on. So it is sort of like guidelines to what we are doing in class for me."

Do you feel like instruction is helpful, that it matches the targets and your needs?

"Usually instruction is on topic. Some things are a smaller part of it (the target) and don't make as much sense (at first), then once we learn the smaller steps within the target, after we learn those, it makes sense."

Do you feel like instruction comes just when you need it?

"I like how we learn something and then the next target has to do with it, but it is a new thing too. It is related and we are learning more information. We know part of it, and then we learn more."

What about your confidence as a scientist—do you feel more confident this year, the same, less?

"If you have met it (the target), it feels good. If you haven't met it then you feel a little confused . . . but then it is easy because the targets get them confused and then they go for help."

Liza and I were able to analyze these student reflections to determine what part of her implementation was going well, and where she wanted to continue to refine her approach. It is important to have information like this to consider at the end of the process.

Number of Steps and Timing

There is no great rule about how many steps a project needs, or how long a step should be. Just think about how you will go about implementing this work, and you will probably see some natural steps to your process.

What's the New Learning? Identifying Learning Targets

Once you determine the scope of the first step, it is important to identify the new learning in this step for both teacher and students. It is easy to forget to identify what we need to learn. In the case of the continuing student collaboration example, the teacher targets for the first step might be . . .

- I can observe and offer descriptive feedback to students as they work collaboratively.

- I can help students identify roles to play that promote quality collaboration.

- I can teach students to monitor their own contributing or distracting behavior.

- I can teach students to lead groups and give one another feedback on participation in collaborative work.

These targets describe what I will need to know and be able to do, in order to implement the plan with quality.

It is obviously also important to identify learning targets for students. In the case of our collaboration example, these learning targets will not replace the current set of content or skill learning targets students are working toward; they will become additional, daily targets, used to help students know what good collaboration may look like as they engage in problem solving. For this example, initial student learning targets might be . . .

- I can demonstrate characteristics of quality collaboration.

- I can stop halfway through collaborative work time, evaluate my participation so far, and make plans for improved collaboration in the second half.

- I can take on the role of: organizer, note-taker, time-checker, or leader.

In a later step in the plan, my students and I may progress to working on these targets:

Me	Learning Target
	• I can explain when collaborating is helpful to me as a thinker and worker.
	• I can articulate characteristics of quality collaboration.
	• I can model characteristics of quality collaboration.
My Students	Learning Target
	• I can explain when collaboration is helpful to me as a thinker and worker.
	• I can identify choices and behaviors that make it hard to collaborate when we are trying to solve problems.
	• I can explain what quality collaboration looks like.

Actions

Once you are clear about what you and your students are trying to learn in this step of implementation, you can map out the key actions for both you and your students. So, using the targets I identified for myself above, a few key actions for me might be . . .

Establish a new purpose for collaboration:

• Share with students that I think collaboration is really special and helpful when we use it in the right circumstances and when we practice how to do it well. Share with students that I wonder how often I have asked them to collaborate to understand something difficult versus how often I have asked them to work together to complete tasks.

• Share example of collaboration from my life. Be sure to identify an example in which I was in a problem-solving situation, and I was working with people I had a lot of practice collaborating with. Introduce the term *colleague*: people you work with to get the job done.

• Ask students to pair share about a time when they were part of good, meaty, problem-solving collaboration. Listen to their examples.

• Introduce a difficult math problem-solving task. Ask if they think this is one worthy of collaboration.

Begin to establish a vision of quality collaboration using a few rounds of pair share:

- Ask students to think about what they could do to learn from colleagues while collaborating; then share and track on chart paper.

- Add any necessary suggestions to the recommended lists.

- Ask students which behaviors would get in the way and make it hard for us to be successful collaborators; then share and track on chart paper.

- Add any necessary cautionary notes to the appropriate list.

Release to try collaborating on math problem with a partner. We will build up to larger groups of colleagues. Observe and give feedback; track trends to report out.

And if the student learning targets are those indicated above, a few key actions for students might be . . .

- Generate ideas with my partner about what good and bad collaboration looks like.

- Listen to the ideas my colleagues share in the discussion.

- Try to be a good collaborator when we go to work with our partner on the math problem.

Figure 5.6 displays how that might play out in a planning template.

Figure 5.6 Planning Template (Example: Collaboration)

Step# 1 _____   Estimated Timing: 10/1/14–10/2/14

Me	Learning Target	Teacher Actions
	• I can explain when collaborating is helpful to me as a thinker and worker. • I can articulate characteristics of quality collaboration.	Establish new purpose for collaboration: • Share with students that I think collaboration is really special and helpful when we use it in the right circumstances and when we practice how to do it well. Share with students that I wonder how often I have asked them to collaborate to understand something difficult versus how often I have asked them to work together to complete tasks.

- I can model characteristics of quality collaboration.

- Share example of collaboration from my life. Be sure to identify an example in which I was in a problem-solving situation, and I was working with people I had a lot of practice collaborating with. Introduce the term "colleague": people you work with to get the job done.
- Ask students to pair share about a time when they were part of a good, meaty, problem-solving collaboration. Listen to their examples.
- Introduce difficult math problem-solving task. Ask if they think this is one worthy of collaboration.

Begin to establish a vision of quality collaboration through a few rounds of pair share:

- Ask students to think about what they could do to learn from colleagues while collaborating; then share and track on chart paper.
- Ask students to think about what they could do to help colleagues learn with collaborating; then share and track on chart paper.
- Add any necessary suggestions to the recommended lists.
- Ask students which behaviors would get in the way and make it hard for us to be successful collaborators; then share and track on chart paper.
- Add any necessary cautionary notes to the appropriate list.

Release to try collaborating on math problem with a partner. We will build up to larger groups of colleagues. Observe and give feedback; track trends to report out.

continues

Figure 5.6 Planning Template (Example: Collaboration), *cont.*

My Students	Learning Target	Student Actions
	• I can explain when collaboration is helpful to me as a thinker and worker. • I can identify choices and behaviors that make it hard to collaborate when we are trying to solve problems. • I can explain what quality collaboration looks like.	• Generate ideas with my partner about what good and bad collaboration looks like. • Listen to the ideas my colleagues share in the discussion. • Try to be a good collaborator when we go to work with our partner on the math problem.

Indicators of Success:

After thinking through the ideas brainstormed in the Data Collection grid, I think I need a very clear and short list of quality collaboration behaviors that I can use to

- teach the students who will help demonstrate collaboration
- label what the students do in their demonstration
- give all students feedback as they collaborate
- guide students' self-assessment.

As students get better and better at collaborating, it seems like changes or additions to the list might be necessary, but I think having a strong, short list to start out with is the right way to go. So, in the first step of the plan, quality collaboration behaviors will include:

> The Data Collection grid (Figure 5.2) was a brainstorm of success indicators for the entire strategy. Now it is time to decide exactly which indicators you will look for as you execute each step of the plan. In terms of mindset, this is a good time to remember to be measured. Trying to track indicators that are hard to capture, or trying to track too many indicators may compromise the quality of overall execution of the plan.

- trying to take turns instead of talking over one another
- posing questions to their group
- nodding their heads in agreement with their peers, or shaking their heads in disagreement
- repeating good ideas they heard from their peers
- disagreeing respectfully.

I also want to give students a warm-up in this part of the plan that asks them what collaboration is and what it looks like. The exit ticket to compare to it will come in a later part. I do not expect to see changes in the numbers of students demonstrating strong understanding of problem solving in individual work that follows collaborative work yet . . . that will be a measure in steps two or three.

Tools and Resources Needed:

- Observation form for me and colleagues to use to track quality collaboration.
- Self-assessment or reflection tool for individuals and small groups.
- Write-up of the problem-solving task and whatever supporting materials they need. I need to dig into end-of-unit questions to see if I can find a math application worthy of this kind of collaborative work.

Knowing the actions for both teacher and student, as well as which indicators of success will be used in this step, it is now possible to identify all of the tools or resources needed to implement this step. Identify all tools as well as any arrangements to be made with colleagues here. Also consider whether the initial timeline will work, given the amount of tool or resource preparation needed.

Monitoring Notes:

After implementing each step in the plan, track key information about measures of success. Also note any other unanticipated positive or negative outcomes. After implementing multiple steps, it will be important to look back at these notes to evaluate the overall effectiveness of the strategy.

(filled in as you implement Step 1)

Plan Steps and Build Tools

Now that you've seen one model of what this can look like, take a moment and think through the plan and tools that you'll need.

Step# _____		Estimated Timing:
Me	Learning Target •	Teacher Actions •
My Students	Learning Target •	Student Actions •

Indicators of Success:

I might observe students . . .

My students may say things like . . .

Student work may change to . . .

Tools and Resources Needed:

Monitoring Notes:

There is no magic number of steps and no universal truth regarding the grain size of each step you identify in your plan. In project planning with teachers over the years, I have found that some people really like granularity, and other people prefer to plan in one big step. Whatever breakdown works for you is great. General advice is to go only as detailed as is helpful to you, and pay close attention to indicators of success, so it will be easier to monitor progress and know if you are on track when you begin to implement.

6 Implement, Monitor, Analyze, and Share

Phase, Time, and Tasks of Education Innovation

Phase of the Work	Estimated Timeframe	Tasks
Implementation and Monitoring	Between 2 and 10 weeks	• Try it. • Gather information and monitor results.
Analysis	2 hours	• Evaluate results with colleagues.
Impact	Timing depends on result	Based on results do one of these three things: 1. If results are bad, analyze the work and rationale to understand why it failed, and never do it or other things with those bad premises again. Share that learning with your colleagues to prevent them from the same failure. 2. If the results are mixed, analyze to understand what worked and didn't. Revisit rationale to see if it still holds up. Try to fix it and repeat the process. 3. If the results were positive, figure out how to share it with your colleagues so they can benefit from your smart ideas and good work.

Excerpt from main table on page 35

The goal of this phase is to learn. By following the step-by-step plan we created and by monitoring to see what it yields, we are learning how to do something different, and hopefully better, in our practice.

Just a couple of reminders about mindset as this phase is executed.

This is an important time to remember to let learning trump ego. Consider opening up your classroom during this phase, so that colleagues can help you monitor. Consider sharing with your students what you are trying and why, so they can participate in evaluating how well the strategy is working. If the first few days aren't as smooth as you hoped, be humble and reflective.

This is also an important time to remember not to let great be the enemy of good. Implementing something that is 80 percent right is the fastest way figure out the last 20 percent. With this approach, any project has the potential to offer a few bumps and therefore offer us an opportunity to learn from failure. It is important to be committed to the learning; doing so puts a person in the right frame of mind to be able to use early failures to figure out the last 20 percent.

Lastly, it is an important time to be measured by looking for those small observable changes and making note of the impact you see along the way. There is a section to track key findings in progress monitoring at the bottom of the step-by-step planning tool. It is important to track this information while implementing. In the analysis phase, these notes from each step in the project will be important. Seeing those small indicators of impact is also an important way to stay motivated and sustain focus through the effort of implementing and monitoring.

Evaluate Results with Colleagues

The basic task here is pretty straightforward; this is the time to compare all of the observed and collected data about impact and compare it to the goal(s) of the project. More precisely, the task here is to look back at observation notes, ask colleagues to share their observations, and review the contents of interviews or surveys conducted with students—identifying patterns among those different sources of information to determine whether this strategy was effective.

In our example, we would probably begin by closely examining observations of student behaviors in collaboration experiences. Over time, did the students' frequency of turn taking, question asking, head nodding, and so on, increase?

Mindset reminder: this is a time when learning trumping ego is really, really important. Sharing successes or failures with your colleagues can feel uncomfortable. For each of us, our personality and our relationships with our colleagues dramatically shape how this step in the process will feel. For some of us, receiving positive attention from our peers for having taken a risk and developed something pretty great is unsettling. Enduring deeply critical feedback can also be difficult. If as a community of doers and learners we can all stay focused on learning, we can have productive, critical, and analytical conversations. That is the goal at this stage in the process.

When it is time to share learning, it is important to be sure that the teacher innovators who are presenting their learning and their colleagues are ready to participate in a way that maximizes learning. This means remembering the characteristics of classrooms that promote intellectual risk-taking and the rules of play for an innovation mindset.

Each rule of play suggests norms for both the teacher innovators and their colleagues to follow when innovation findings are presented.

Rules of Play for an Innovation Mindset

1. Learning Trumps Ego:

Being humble, open, and honest with ourselves and colleagues is an essential component to learning as a community. It also helps us learn faster.

For the teacher innovator(s) . . .	For their colleagues . . .
• If you have positive findings, present with continued openness to question and critique. Responsible colleagues will need to dig in deep to understand and trust enough to try implementing in their classrooms.	• If a colleague shares thinking that isn't new to you, please don't point that out or explain how you discovered that in the past. It does more to promote you than to promote learning.
• If you have mixed or failed findings to share, present with honesty and confidence. Your colleagues trust that you are a good teacher who was willing to take a risk to make something great.	• Instead, ask questions about where he or she is thinking of going next, and offer a few ideas for next steps.
	• When asking critical questions, try to find ways to express to your colleague that you trust his or her capacity as a teacher.
	• Be open to a colleague's discovery that is counter to your current understanding, and listen carefully; there might be powerful learning there.
	• Ask questions about implementation. Really dig to find out how he or she did what he or she did.
	• Ask questions about which students or types of students were most dramatically impacted.

2. Don't Let Great Be the Enemy of Good:

When we are willing to trust our expertise and try implementing things when they are really good, maybe 80 percent of the way there, rather than waiting to make them perfect, we end up finding perfect faster. When we try to figure out the remaining 20 percent by running through multiple scenarios in our minds, or creating a dozen different permutations of our idea, we may feel more certain but are still very unlikely to have it 100 percent right.

For the teacher innovator(s) . . .	For their colleagues . . .
• If you have positive findings, but you aren't sure you have perfected your strategy, share it with confidence.	• If what you hear your colleague present isn't perfection, try to listen and identify the potential.
• Consider asking your colleagues to help you further refine the strategy.	• Be open to helping further develop a strategy, and if relevant to problems in your classroom, trying the strategy yourself.
• Consider asking your colleagues to try your strategy so you can learn more together.	

3. Be Measured:

Be disciplined about how much you take on and disciplined in how carefully you implement the Responsible Innovation Process.

For the teacher innovator(s) . . .	For their colleagues . . .
• Stick to your plans for measuring effectiveness. If the plan didn't produce the results you predicted, analyze rather than avoid that in presentation.	• There is only so much feedback a person can use at once. Reflect before sharing feedback so you ensure that the most important ideas get real consideration.
• Stick to your timeline and present your findings even if you think you still have more to try and learn.	

This set of norms is really just a starting place. All groups of colleagues need to discuss their sensitivities and communication styles. There are good common norms about taking turns talking and demonstration of listening. Those are good too. I encourage groups of colleagues to use this and other norms they have for other kinds of professional collaboration and generate their own norms to promote intellectual risk-taking in both classroom and staff room environments.

Once you gather together and establish norms, you are ready to evaluate. Even if everything goes smoothly, it will still be unlikely that a project yields a clear comprehensive success or failure. So, it may be useful to determine the impact of smaller aspects of the strategy or implementation (see Figure 6.1).

What Do I Do with the Results?

Based on results, do one of these three things: share lessons learned from failure, devise a revised strategy, or plan for sharing and scaling the strategy.

Sometimes it may seem smart to respond in a couple of different ways for different aspects of a strategy. For each lesson learned, whether it was a success, partial success, or failure, a run through the decision-making tree in Figure 6.2 may be helpful in determining how to use the lessons learned in the project to improve practice.

Whether we find ourselves nervous to admit failures or uncomfortable sharing successes, we must overcome those fears and share our learning. In a culture in which we are given permission to be inventive, a strong practice of learning from one another is required to accelerate our collective effectiveness and maintain trust.

Figure 6.1 Critical Questions for Evaluation

- Who benefited most from this strategy? How do we know? Why do we think that is true?

- Who benefited least from this strategy? How do we know? Why do we think that is true?

- Were there any unanticipated negative consequences of this strategy? Could they be mitigated easily?

- Were there any unanticipated positive consequences? Why did those happen?

- Was there a step in the process where things seemed to click? Was that because of the accumulated skills from previous steps, or was that step more important to the success of the strategy than others?

- Was there a step in the process that seemed to hold things up or get students stuck? Why was that so? Is there a better way to execute that step in the plan?

- Did some tools work better than others? What were the characteristics of the most effective tools?

Figure 6.2 Did It Work?

When Should You Convert Existing Practices?

To further clarify the idea of converting, there are a few quick examples below of changes that could be made to common classroom processes. I am sure many readers will be familiar with the suggestions in these examples. While reading these examples, try to see this practice from a student's perspective, and think about how each of these changes would help you be the owner of your learning.

- What about this would help you know where you stand or relate effort and progress?

- What about this example would empower you to make decisions about what effort you need to exert, or support you need to find, to figure out the parts you are currently missing?

| **Instead of** assigning a series of readings for homework and expecting everyone to read everything assigned each week, help students make smart choices about how to spend their at-home study time. | **Convert:**
• Ask students to reflect on recent work and identify gaps and areas of interest related to the learning target for the week.
• Then introduce a set of four or five readings aimed at different components of the learning target.
• Ask students to commit on Monday to what they will read and what they hope to get from reading it. On Friday students turn in a paragraph summarizing key findings from each text they read at home. |

Instead of scheduling students into an unstructured study hall, help them be proactive about setting goals, getting support, and measuring progress.	**Convert:** • Ask students to keep notes in a particular place in their planner indicating what they need to work on in study hall. • Facilitate a process at the beginning of study hall in which students identify what they are working on and whether time with a peer on that topic would be helpful. Allow students to regroup so they are sitting with or near others interested in doing the same work. • At the end of study hall, ask students to track in their planner what they got done and what they need to do at home.
Instead of teachers being the presenters of information about school success in parent-teacher conferences, consider teaching students to present to parents summary information about both their effort and progress in student-led conferences.	• Help students pull together a summary of their progress toward targets. Ideally this is supported by standards-based grading or a portfolio system. But it is possible in any system in which students have consistently received feedback connected to learning targets. • Work with students to establish criteria for a quality and persuasive presentation about their progress. • Model strong and weak presentations. • Have students practice with one another. • Hold student-led conferences.
Instead of grading and returning work to then be sent home or thrown away, build a portfolio system with students that houses their work along with feedback.	• At the beginning of a study of a set of learning targets, ask students to determine what they already know and can do with respect to these targets. • As students do work toward this set of targets, have them collect formative and summative pieces of work in a folder, binder, or electronic environment. • Before moving from one set of learning targets to another, ask students to reflect back on their progress toward the targets. Did they hit them? What evidence do they have to support their assessment? Add that reflection to their collection of formative and summative pieces of work in their portfolio. • At quarters, semesters, or in preparation for student-led conferences—ask students to look back at how their work and understanding has changed.

I've shared these examples in hope that they inspire you to think differently about some other practice in your classroom. This might lead you to identify some problems that you can solve through conversion.

Now that you have a sense of possibility, let's explore the strategy of conversion in a bit more depth.

Retuning Instructional Protocols

Instructional protocols are tools that give groups of students (or adults) clear ways to share, discuss, critique, or analyze a text or idea. Protocols dictate how we participate in discussion and, in doing so, help people engage in meaningful, focused, balanced, and accessible dialogue. You have probably used protocols before; some are very common and built into a range of published curricula. Protocols range from simple things—like Think, Pair, Share—to complex, independently facilitated extended dialogue in scored discussions or Socratic seminars.

A USEFUL RESOURCE ON PROTOCOLS

If you are new to the use of protocols and are looking for a good introduction, I recommend the National School Reform Faculty website. This URL goes straight to their list of protocols. www.nsrfharmony.org/protocol/a_z.html.

Even without any conversion, protocols can be excellent tools to support students in working together to investigate, analyze connections, and consider a range of perspectives. With a small adjustment regarding the process for reflecting on participation, protocols can also be a great way to help students see who they are as a collaborator and member of a group.

Protocol Conversion Example: Scored Discussion

A scored discussion is a protocol that asks students to explore different perspectives. In her seventh-grade language arts class, Sonia Rau and her students study a topical issue, so that they can analyze nonfiction text and take a stand to write persuasive papers. Sonia selected type 2 diabetes for their topic of study. She made this decision for two reasons: their school community is heavily impacted by diabetes, and the students are studying the human body in science. Sonia was also pleased to find that there were a large number of articles written at or near the students' reading level on this topic.

Let's imagine that Sonia's students have just read two articles describing two very different approaches to diabetes treatment. The first article describes what is thought of as traditional diabetes treatment, which involved close blood glucose monitoring and injected insulin. The second article suggests that a surgical procedure could be used to treat diabetes. Both articles identify current research that supports the method described in the article. Each article also lays out the benefits and risks of the approach to treatment.

Let's examine two scenarios that Sonia could follow with the scored discussion protocol: Scenario A uses the scored discussion protocol as it is; in Scenario B Sonia converts her use of the same protocol to help her students develop capacity as proactive professionals. In her real classroom, Sonia sometimes used this protocol in both of these ways.

In Scenario A, Sonia planned to use the scored discussion protocol only as a way to help students deepen their understanding of the content. That would be a great reason to use a discussion protocol, and many classrooms would be improved just by using protocols for this purpose and in this way. But in Scenario B, Sonia had been using protocols long enough to notice some other nice side effects: students becoming more participatory, students feeling comfortable questioning one another, students demonstrating a high level of preparation and responsibility for their learning. Having noticed some of those benefits, she designs a lesson to really leverage use of the protocol to teach her students how to be proactive professionals.

	Scenario A: *Sonia uses protocol to deepen content understanding.*	**Scenario B:** *Sonia plans to use protocol to build content knowledge and build their capacity to be proactive professionals.*
What Sonia thinks about and has in mind as she plans	Sonia understands that protocols are a great way to get kids talking about the content and make class interesting. She selects scored discussion because it offers some structure and accountability for participation, which makes her feel more comfortable in her management.	Sonia understands that when students have to use evidence to support their opinion, they have to think like scholars. She also understands that discussions, especially those where her students disagree with one another, are engaging. She also knows that she needs to require and teach students to take an active role in her classroom and their learning. She has been thinking about that last point a lot in the last few weeks, as she has seen some students step up as leaders in her room and others stay passive, or even become more passive.

Learning target(s) for students	• I can evaluate evidence to decide which diabetes treatment is the best.	• I can evaluate evidence to decide which diabetes treatment is the best.
		• I can actively participate in scored discussion.
		  • This means I do my part to push the discussion forward.
		  • This means I use the discussion to help me deepen my own understanding

continues

	Scenario A: *Sonia uses protocol to deepen content understanding.*	**Scenario B:** *Sonia plans to use protocol to build content knowledge and build their capacity to be proactive professionals.*
What Sonia asks students to do to prepare for the scored discussion	Write down which treatment you think is the best, and three reasons why. That is your ticket to participate in the discussion. Sonia shows the rubric on the document camera and reminds them that she will be scoring their participation.	Decide which treatment is best, then find at least three pieces of evidence in the text that support your idea. If you can, find a piece of support in the opposing article. When they are done with that, Sonia asks them to do one more thing . . . Take a look at the scored discussion rubric. I want you to pay special attention to two criteria: 1. **Use of evidence.** You should be prepared to do that well. I will be looking for how frequently and easily you can refer to the text to support your ideas. 2. **Active participant.** Part of what we are working on right now is being active learners—scholars who take charge of their learning. I will be looking for each of you to listen actively and add in relevant comments that build on what has been discussed, push the conversation forward, and use this opportunity to deepen your own understanding of the diabetes treatment options. Before we start, I want you to set a specific goal for yourself regarding active participation and write it down on the same paper where you have made note of the sections of text you plan to refer to. We will also quickly share out these goals before we begin.
What happens in the discussion	• The students get set and Sonia states the prompt: Which method is the best, and why?	• Students begin by sharing their goal with a partner sitting next to them. • Sonia reminds them to pay attention to their goal and see what they can do to demonstrate active participation. Then she states the prompt: Which method is best, and what evidence do you have to support that perspective?

| **What happens in the discussion, *cont.*** | • Students are ready to share their opinions. They have ideas to back them up. They take turns saying their opinion and their reasons for their opinion. They frequently use transitions like, "I agree with you because . . ." or "I disagree with you because." Each article is referred to as having said certain things, but students do not read quotes from the article or point out where their idea could be found by others as they speak.
• Students are engaged, and many of them contribute. Some are quiet but do not disturb the conversation.
• After the discussion, students are asked to revisit their notes and make note of either how their opinion changed and what evidence persuaded them to change, or what other evidence they heard to further support their unchanged opinion.
• In debrief, a few students are cold-called to share their notes about how their opinion has changed or evidence deepened. | • When students are ready to share, they take turns sharing their perspectives and quoting the text and explaining why those quotes support their perspective. Students ask one another questions about why they thought that quote from the text was strong evidence and suggest other points of strong evidence or disagree about interpretation of quotes from the text. Students frequently use transitions like, "I agree with you, but this part of the text is what really persuaded me"; "I disagree with you, I don't think that quote means that, because I think it is saying . . ." Students are pointing to the text, flipping pages back and forth as they present ideas and as they listen to peers.
• Students are engaged, and as the discussion ends, the teacher gives them a reminder that they are nearly out of time and asks students to look at their active participation goals to see if there is anything they should do before time is up.
• A few more students share, including some who had been quiet.
• The teacher ends the discussion.
• Students are first asked to revisit their notes and make note of either how their opinion changed and what evidence persuaded them to change—or what other evidence they heard to further support their unchanged opinion.
• Students are then asked to evaluate their performance on the two criteria. They are also asked to identify what they saw peers do to demonstrate active participation.
• There are then three steps to the debrief.
  1. A few students are cold-called to share their notes about how their opinion has changed or evidence deepened.
  2. Students give the teacher a thumbs up or down to indicate whether they think they reached each target.
  3. The teacher asks them to identify what they saw their peers do to demonstrate active participation. The teacher tracks these actions on chart paper, so they can be reviewed before their next scored discussion to support students in setting goals for their participation. |

continues

	Scenario A: *Sonia uses protocol to deepen content understanding.*	**Scenario B:** *Sonia plans to use protocol to build content knowledge and build their capacity to be proactive professionals.*
At the end of the discussion, what did students get?	• Students got to hear what others thought about the issue. • They also had the chance to put their ideas out there and see if others thought in similar ways. • Students had a chance to share their opinion in a large venue and practice speaking about academic content. • Students had practice providing a rationale for their opinions, which prepares them for persuasive writing. • Students had the opportunity to revise their thinking based on ideas and evidence shared in the discussion.	• Students got to hear what others thought about the issue. • They also had the chance to put their ideas out there and see if others agreed with their use of evidence. • Students had a chance to share their opinion in a large venue and practice speaking about academic content. • Students had practice justifying their opinion by citing and interpreting information provided in each text, which prepares them for persuasive writing. • Students had the opportunity to revise their thinking based on ideas and evidence shared in the discussion. • Students had the responsibility to participate actively and help in seeing what that would look like. If they didn't participate with quality today, they got a vision of how they can do that next time.

Consider the following questions as you analyze these two scenarios: Think about what the teacher in each scenario made explicit and clear to students. How might that affect student participation in each classroom?

Practically speaking, how feasible is it for you to make and sustain a change like this?

This example illustrates a number of things; one of these is how silly it is to add collaboration classes or programs onto our existing way of doing school. Rather than creating "collaboration time" or "justification time" in the day or week, teachers can convert practices to make collaboration and justification of ideas part of learning other content. As we work to prepare our students for this global, plugged-in, integrated, collaborative, project-driven society and economy, we need to redesign the most basic aspects of how we do school, so that doing school looks and feels a lot like being an adult in the twenty-first century.

So, how does a teacher go from Scenario A to B and beyond? To find out, I interviewed Sonia about her experiences implementing the use of protocols.

What did the first scored discussion look like?

"The first time, I didn't really adapt it (the rubric) for my classroom. I kept the score sheet I was given. But then I realized that 'put downs' wasn't worth having on the rubric. That didn't match my students."

"On the positive side, we were having a great discussion but not tied too tightly to the text. But that first time was still meeting my goals."

"Most kids bought in early. Kids who think of themselves as more freethinking didn't buy in as fast; I can understand that. I feel that way when they (protocols) are given to me too. But every time I think that, by the end, I think it is really helpful."

As you can tell from her comments above, Sonia had a modest goal in mind when they began; she wanted to give her students a controlled way to have a great discussion. Even in this early implementation, most kids, including many beyond those who are naturally proactive students, bought in and tried to participate with quality in the discussion. Sonia achieved her initial goal, and she identified what would need to change to really get everything she could out of scored discussion.

Being able to anticipate the early bumps is essential to being able to problem-solve your way through early efforts and lead your class into fluent implementation. Take a moment to think about how your students might respond to participating in a scored discussion.

What about scored discussion would be natural or unnatural to them?

Can you anticipate the disappointments you and your class might experience in your first try?

Continued Implementation

Sonia saw potential in her initial effort and, as a result, she continued to deepen her use of scored discussion with her students throughout the school year.

How has your use of scored discussions changed over time?
"Another teacher was working on accountable talk, and I picked that up and added that to our rubric. That shared practice really moved us forward."

"As I implemented I became less rigid. I flexed the rubric, and eventually we did it enough that students became fluent, so that now we don't have to have the rubric."

"I think the key in middle school is frequency—just doing it over and over."

How has student use and engagement in scored discussion changed over time?
"Kids are way more familiar with it now; they have seen what it looks like to pose a question to the group and are more comfortable with it. They ask better questions. . . . They refer to what someone said and ask a specific question. We have moved beyond, 'What do you think?'"

"Engagement has improved. Kids who were shy became familiar. I tracked who was participating, saying we need more names, and over time students started to notice that and invite one another to the discussion. The simplicity of the protocol makes it easy for them to get good at it. They drive what they want to talk about now and guide the discussion where it needs to go."

"My dominating people are still dominating; that is still the way it is. But I have noticed kids who are shy or reluctant raise hands."

"It is more fluid now. When we had a discussion the other day, an impromptu discussion about something, I didn't expect a lot of hands, but I had a lot of them. Some of the same behaviors from scored discussion started happening naturally in a whole-group discussion."

How and why did those changes happen?
"Getting in the moment of feedback helps. Tracking who has spoken up, referring to the rubric and scoring kids. . . . Gentle teacher and peer feedback along the way also helps."

"I think that being scored is really important. Also, connecting classroom positive reinforcement systems to the scores students receive in discussion."

You have no doubt noticed all kinds of interesting things about how this progressed for Sonia and her students. I want to highlight three ideas that stood out to me as I talked with Sonia.

▩ First: The Power of Teacher Partners

All of the practices in this book are powerful when used by any individual teacher, but that power is magnified when teams of teachers agree to implement practices together. Sonia didn't have to teach her students about accountable talk; her colleague did that for her. She just took language her students were familiar with and added it to her rubric. This kind of shared practice makes learning more efficient and deepens students' use of strategies.

▩ Second: Trust, Capacity, and Confidence Grow Together

Sonia began this effort because she wanted structure and control, but along the way she learned to trust her students and give them greater latitude. The value of this kind of relationship between teacher and students cannot be overstated. Notice how Sonia and her students build both capacity and trust over time.

- Sonia gave her students a structured way to try to be more independent and collaborative, knowing that they wouldn't initially do it very well.

- Sonia provided feedback and persisted through early attempts, giving her students a chance to demonstrate high levels of performance.

- Her students improved. They took responsibility for participating and became more sophisticated in how they shared, asked questions, and justified their ideas.

- Sonia watched closely and noticed incremental changes in their skill and pointed out those changes to her students.

- Students noticed their growth over time so that their confidence grew parallel to their competence.

- Because she saw those changes, Sonia trusted her students to run their discussions with increasing independence, eventually backing out of her role as vocal participation tracker.

▩ Third: Productive Persistence = Frequency + Feedback

If Sonia had tried to persist by doing scored discussions once per quarter, her students wouldn't have made this kind of progress. Practice is a thing that must be done regularly so students notice progress and build momentum, so they associate practicing with getting better. Likewise, if she hadn't provided students with immediate feedback and then taught them to give immediate feedback to one another, they wouldn't have grown as they did. Both frequency and feedback are required to make sticking with this practice, or any other practice, worthwhile.

In-Depth Look at Maximizing Use of Assessment for Learning Practices

The key idea of assessment for learning is to do everything possible to help students assess, track, and assign meaning to their performance and progress over time. Doing so helps students build their capacity as both proactive learners and professionals.

It may be helpful here to briefly reflect on how you learned that there was a positive correlation between your effort and your progress? When did you learn that if you try, work hard, and stick with something, you get better at it? If someone else helped you learn about that relationship, how did they do it?

In their book *Classroom Assessment for Student Learning: Doing It Right—Using It Well*, Stiggins et al. (2006) identify seven components of assessment for learning. (Available at http://ati.pearson.com/downloads/chapters/7%20Strats%20Ch%201.pdf.)[1]

> Strategy 1: Provide students with a clear and understandable vision of the learning target.
> Strategy 2: Use examples and models of strong and weak work.
> Strategy 3: Offer regular descriptive feedback.
> Strategy 4: Teach students to self-assess and set goals.
> Strategy 5: Design lessons to focus on one learning target or aspect of quality at a time.
> Strategy 6: Teach students focused revision.
> Strategy 7: Engage students in self-reflection, and let them keep track of and share their learning.

They describe these strategies as the way that teachers can help students know where they are going, how close or far they are from that destination, and what they can do to close that gap.

I think this is a solid construct for evaluating current practice. We can turn each of these intentions into questions.

- What have I done to make the intended learning, the destination for this work, clear to my students?

- What have I done, at the beginning and ongoing, to help students see how close or far they are from that destination?

- What have I done to help students know how to get to the destination and close that gap?

---

[1] Stiggins, Rick J.; Arter, Judith A.; Chappuis, Jan; Chappuis, Steve, *Classroom Assessment for Student Learning: Doing It Right—Using It Well*, First Edition © 2006. Printed and electronically reproduced by permission of Pearson Education, Inc., Upper Saddle River, New Jersey.

To maximize proactive benefits, I would add one question to this construct: Did I do those things in a way that gave a heavy lift in terms of thinking to my students? In other words . . .

- What have students done to get a clear picture of the intended learning?

- What have students done to get an accurate picture of how close or far they are from our intended destination?

- What choices have students made to engage in work, practice, or instruction to help them get closer to our intended destination?

Initial Implementation

To learn more about how these ideas play out in practice, I interviewed Heather White. She was teaching second-grade girls in Cleveland, Ohio, when we talked.

We began by discussing why she started using assessment for learning practices. Heather had, fortunately or unfortunately, been my student teacher. So, although she had moved away from Colorado to live in Cleveland, she remained in touch with me and others from our former school who were digging into Rick Stiggins and Assessment for Learning. Her conversations with colleagues on the topic struck a chord with Heather.

"I have always believed in putting ownership for learning on the shoulders of students. That is the root of lifelong learning. If students can take responsibility for their learning, and see it as theirs, then their learning is a thing that no one else is in charge of. That is where my interest started."

"Then that sort of grew to how can it be more deliberate—how can I be more transparent with my students about what exactly I want them to learn and whether they have been successful or not?"

What did your first attempts to implement assessment for learning look like?
"Before I started, the hardest part was narrowing it down. What is most important to learn right now in their second-grade lives? It could be a lot of things. The targets need to be realistic, but I also need to be sure they are on track to be ready for third grade. Also—right now, we are doing a genre study with Native American legends, connecting to a unit on Native American culture, history, and beliefs. So—I need to figure out what the most important aspects of writing are in that genre. The standards don't tell you that; you have to analyze literature and find that on your own, which is hard."

"In the beginning, I would mostly do things like say, 'This is our learning target, and here's what you are going to learn from this project.' At other times I would have them read like a writer, and then take their observations about what makes a successful piece of writing and use that to generate the specific targets."

"Another early example was a punctuation study, just reading a bunch of picture books and noticing things about how the author was using punctuation. A lot of them never noticed what an ellipsis was, or that it was called an ellipsis. After we noticed the ellipses together, then they all began to notice that authors used them a lot. Then they started noticing other things that authors did with punctuation. It was short and concrete."

"When I asked them to write a short piece using interesting punctuation—there were varying levels of success in terms of getting beyond commas and ellipses—but that told me that is where they are—they could and did use those basic pieces of punctuation correctly. They didn't try too many new things, but it was the first time I saw them transfer things they found when reading like a writer, into their writing."

You can hear already that Heather had a reasonable initial outcome in mind; she wanted to see her students analyze models to get a vision of what reaching the target looks like and to identify new strategies for using punctuation. Then she wanted to see at least some of that show up in their writing. This is a good example of an early success measure. But for Heather, since her ultimate goal was to increase students' ownership of their learning, to help them be proactive learners, she needed to take things further.

Continued Implementation

Where did you and your students go next with assessment for learning?
"Our next step was that I provided them with the long-term target, in the case of the legend project, 'I can write a successful legend,' and then we analyzed models to generate those specific supporting targets. I had in mind that we needed to notice things about: purpose of legends, organizational structure, the components of quest or journey stories, common roles (tricksters, heroes, etc.), and aspects of culture that we could see in the characters (both animal and human), setting, central problem, discussions of character, spirit, death, and redemption. I selected models that illustrated these different components of legends in different ways."

How did that go?

"It was good because they noticed all the things I wanted them to notice. You sort of have to trust that kids are going to pick up on what you want them to pick up on. It was more powerful that they came up with them and that I valued their observations. We talked about how they don't always have to rely on me to decide what is most important. They will be in situations where they will have to determine importance. They can collaborate and figure that out as a group."

You identified a risk when you said you had to trust that kids are going to pick up on key quality criteria. Have they ever missed something important, and if so, how did you handle it?

"Usually what I do is help them see the missing quality or criteria in some other way. Not directly telling them, but using a line of questioning that would have them look more closely at a certain part—something like—this happened in this legend, did it also happen in this one, and this one? . . . It is like helping them through the scavenger hunt; we are making this new discovery together. I think having clear learning targets enables teachers to ask good questions."

How has student use and engagement with student-driven assessment for learning changed over time?

"As we have continued to do this, one thing that sometimes happens when we study models to get a picture of the intended learning is that they notice things I didn't notice or come up with a way to say something that is spot on and better than how I imagined labeling or describing it. They will come up with it and label it using nonacademic language. Once we all understand, I try to give them the academic label, like a metaphor or simile. They will say it painted a picture. I will ask how. Then I help label for them that the writer uses a comparison to help you get that picture in the reader's mind. That is something good writers do all the time to get you to understand what they are trying to describe."

"Also—now they do a self-assessment after their first draft to determine how successfully they have written a legend. They use that to identify what they have and what they need to add or change to make it include the appropriate components in a clear logical way that makes sense. Then they engage in peer critiques where someone else identifies evidence of meeting the target within their writing—literally highlighting in their draft. Highlighting a peer's text, and letting them highlight yours, is high-level professional collaboration. Sometimes they have to talk it out; sometimes the peer reviewer sees things differently."

What do you see as attainable/natural next steps for you and your students in use of student-driven assessment for learning practices?

"I am in my sixth year of teaching second grade, and I still sometimes over- or underestimate what they are ready to do with this. Our next step is to go further with this in reading. I want to help girls analyze whether their use of a strategy is helping them be successful readers. They know the strategies, they know they should thinking some specific way when they read—now they are ready also to evaluate whether the thinking they did, using the strategy they used, resulted in them making more or better sense of the text."

While listening to Heather, I am sure you noticed a few connections to aspects of proactive learners and professionals. I want to highlight two ideas that stood out to me as I listened to Heather.

■ **First: The Importance of Trusting Students** (This is a repeat for those of you who read the section on protocols.)

By trusting her students to analyze models and identify quality criteria, Heather was able to offer students a clearer, more student-friendly view of the intended learning than she could deliver on her own. So, even if all I cared about was more kids reaching academic outcomes, I would be really interested in what Heather is up to. But in terms of helping her girls develop as proactive learners and collaborators, there is so much more going on here.

Imagine being a student in Heather's classroom.

- You are trusted to analyze models and identify criteria.

- You are trusted to use that information to produce quality writing using ideas and strategies you have never tried before.

- You are trusted to assess your best work against quality criteria.

- You are then trusted to listen to feedback from a peer about your best work and figure out how to use that feedback to make your work better.

- And—you are trusted to offer feedback to a peer to help them improve their work . . .

If you were a student in Heather's room, who would you think has a lot of great ideas—Heather, or you and your peers? Who would you think is responsible for figuring out how to do something well? Who would you think is a good writer, with expertise to offer to other intrepid writers?

Students in her room couldn't help but feel that they were in charge of their own learning. And, when peer critique is part of the equation, students also feel some responsibility to help others do well too. It is a small, but important, way to practice being a contributing member of a community.

Kids can't learn to be proactive unless we trust them to behave that way.

■ Second: The Importance of Collaborating on Important Things

Group work is not necessarily the same as collaborating. Have you ever been the kid on the group project who just ends up doing things on your own, because you wanted to show the teacher you knew what you were doing, even if the yahoos in your group didn't care about their grade? Or the person in a group who waits for someone to take charge and assign you a task, so you can complete your task and know you are done whether anyone else does their work or not? Kids often demonstrate low-level collaborative skills when the task isn't one that really requires, or dramatically benefits from, collaboration. When members of a team split up tasks to be efficient, they are not collaborating. Collaborating entails interacting with one another, trying together to figure something out in a way that is deeper and better than you could do on your own.

For Heather's young writers, when they assess a friend's writing, they have an important job to do. They are supposed to help their colleague improve their writing. They are going to be held accountable for doing their best job, because they will have to sit down and talk with their colleague about where they agreed and disagreed with their self-assessment. In a classroom with strong culture, peer pressure alone would prevent most kids from going into that conversation without something specific and important to say. Similarly, when one of Heather's students sits down to listen to a colleague and understand why he or she sees some things differently, the student has to listen and consider a different perspective. But there is a legitimate reason to listen and try to understand what students think. Doing so might help them improve their writing.

On both sides of this interaction, students have a good reason to try to work together as real collaborators. This is important collaboration; we should ask students to collaborate only when the chances of achieving the task are greatly enhanced through collaboration. Which also means that if we want to teach students to collaborate, we need to regularly ask questions and give students tasks that are genuinely complex. *(This is great, because that also helps them deepen their skills as learners.)*

So, while it is certainly OK to also have kids work together for other reasons, it is important to clearly label for students when we are asking them to divide and conquer to complete a task versus when we are asking them to collaborate. Otherwise, we risk teaching students that collaborating is doing your individual part with quality, which is very important but is not collaboration.

Taking Use of Student-Driven Assessment for Learning Further

Once students have developed strong model analysis, skill integration, and self-assessment skills, they are ready to make some decisions about what to do based on what they see in that self-assessment. If a student in Heather's class realized that they didn't really have a clear lesson built into their idea for a legend, what do they do next? In advanced implementation of student-driven assessment for learning, the teacher offers students choices for support. Heather might, on a given day in the legend project, offer the following:

- a minilesson on matching the problem to the lesson in your legend

- a small-group discussion led by a peer on how to really help your reader get a picture of your main character in their mind

- the option to go study an example at the "strong models table," where small bins of books are labeled: character, setting, problem-lesson connection, illustrations, and so on.

- the Peer Brainstorm Table, where you can invite a colleague to join you and give you ideas about how to fix whatever you are not satisfied with in your legend right now

When students have options and can make choices, they practice being good independent learners. This practice is a building block in helping students learn how to make good use of their personal networks and the unimaginable number of tutorials on the Internet.

Rethinking Basic Daily Routines

To promote proactive and accountable behavior, we need to rethink the routines that structure our day. The tables below describe common approaches to a number of school and classroom routines and then describe changes we could make to those routines. This list is certainly not a complete list of all of the basic routines of school that might be ready for redesign; it was designed to be illustrative rather than exhaustive.

I am sure that many readers already make great use of routine opportunities. Maybe you will find an idea or two for other opportunities here. Or perhaps something here will spark your thinking about how you might redesign a completely different routine.

As you read, imagine how changes like this, on a daily basis, over the thirteen years students are in school with us, might impact their perception of themselves as learners, professionals, and community members. How can changes in routine help students for whom being proactive is something they are working hard to learn?

Routine: Start of Day in Elementary School Classroom

Common Start-of-Day Routine:	Connections to Proactive Characteristics:
Students come in and sit in a circle, or at desks, and wait quietly for the teacher to start class.	*In this scenario, while this method ensures a calm and controlled start to the day, or class period, it also ensures that students begin their time in a passive role. Students are rewarded for sitting quietly and waiting for directions from their teacher.*
Conversion Example: Students come in and visit the task chart. They have five minutes to complete their task (things like: sharpen pencils or check a book bin to ensure things are sorted appropriately, laying out materials for first lesson on tables/desks). Then they come to the rug to report on task completion. Teacher cold-calls a few students to explain why their job was important to the class.	**Connections to Proactive Characteristics:** *In this example, students begin their day in an active role and doing something that contributes to their community.*
Conversion Example: Students come in, grab clipboards, paper, and pencil, hurry over to the circle, and start working through a set of number-fluency practice problems. When time is up, the teacher posts the correct answers, and students work with a partner to check for accuracy. They record the number correct and total number attempted on their individual math fact charts. In the circle, students use thumbs up or down to indicate whether they were faster than yesterday, then again for whether they got more problems right than yesterday.	**Connections to Proactive Characteristics:** *In this example, students begin their day in an active role, and they have a responsibility to track their progress with this task over time. This helps them practice tracking their progress.*

Routine: Start of Day/Start of Class in Middle or High School Classroom

Common Upper School Start-of-Class Routine:	Connections to Proactive Characteristics:
Students come in, go to lockers as needed, and make their way to first period.	*In this scenario, students' primary responsibility is to avoid commotion and go unnoticed.*
Conversion Example:	**Connections to Proactive Characteristics:**
The day begins with fifteen-minute grade-level or whole-school community meetings in which students have a rotating set of leadership responsibilities.	*In this example, students have a meaningful and visible role in ensuring there is a focused and crisp start to the day. Right away, they are either seeing students be leaders or being leaders themselves.*
Common Example:	**Connections to Proactive Characteristics:**
Students come in and sit at desks or tables and wait quietly for the teacher to start class.	*Like the previous elementary example, while this method ensures a calm and controlled start to each class period, it also ensures that students begin their time in a passive role. Students are rewarded for sitting quietly and waiting for directions from their teacher.*
Conversion Example:	**Connections to Proactive Characteristics:**
When students come in, there is a question on the board and a timer running. The question is a thought-provoking question about their current study in this class. It could be asking students to explain how the work they will do today (outlined in an agenda on the board) will help them make progress toward the long-term goals or guiding questions of their current study in the class. Students have three minutes to respond to the question in their personal notes. When the timer goes off, they talk to a partner to check their thinking. Then the teacher cold-calls a few students to share their ideas, and uses those responses to introduce the lesson for the day.	*The work of identifying and explaining the purpose for daily learning doesn't always have to fall on the teacher. Once students are a little way into a well-constructed study, they can make the connections between small bits of learning, discrete tasks, and the ultimate learning goals of the course, study, or investigation. If they make the connections, they are more likely to feel their daily work has purpose. This is also a great way to practice making intellectual and conceptual connections.*

Routine: Management of Classroom Materials

Common Materials Management Routine:	Connections to Proactive Characteristics:
To maximize time, teachers carefully lay out all of the materials required for an activity before students come into the classroom. At the end of the work, teachers ask students to stack materials neatly on their tables/desks. They will collect and put them away later.	*This process makes good use of time, and models the importance of doing so, but it makes the teacher be the only one responsible for ensuring that efficiency.*
Conversion Example:	**Connections to Proactive Characteristics:**
The teacher has materials for the lesson with them at the front of the room and has taught students quick procedures for distributing and returning materials. When their instruction is done, they obviously look at the clock to be ready. The teacher then says "ready . . . go!" Students launch into their materials-distribution process. Teacher watches and announces the number of seconds it took to distribute materials. Everyone either briefly celebrates or notes a need to do better with materials return later. See video excerpts in "Teach Like a Champion" for examples.	*Instead of removing responsibility for materials from students, teach them to manage them very, very quickly and with quality. Then you still ensure lots of time on academic task and model making great use of time, but you also teach them how to work with others and make great use of time.*

Routine: Announcements

Common Announcements Routine:	Connections to Proactive Characteristics:
A teacher or administrator is responsible for collecting information from colleagues for daily announcements. They organize and deliver announcements each day.	*In this scenario, students can remain relatively invisible and have no responsibility.*
Conversion Example:	**Connections to Proactive Characteristics:**
The school decides that they will only do speaker announcements for information that promotes and supports the culture in their school. All other information goes out in weekly emails to students and families. A teacher or administrator creates a Google doc, or other shared space, for teachers, students, and parents to let them know information for announcements. Each Friday at lunch, a small group of students meet with the teacher or administrator to review information in the Google doc and determine which information to include in announcements that afternoon and again on Monday morning. Other information is built into an email by the teacher or administrator and distributed on Friday afternoon.	*In this example, a small routine is maximized as an instrument of culture, and students are given the responsibility to decide what kind of information and communication is culture building. This could be a responsibility that everyone has for a month in their middle or high school career, so that everyone takes a turn practicing how to communicate in a culture-building way.*

Routine: Handing Back Graded Work or an Assessment

Common Handing Back Work Routine:
Teacher hands back paper and shares what meaning they took from the assessment: this test showed me that as a group you are ready for our next step—or—this exit ticket showed me that there are some of you who need more instruction and some of you who are ready to move on. The teacher then uses that description of performance to introduce the next steps and what will happen in class today.

Connections to Proactive Characteristics:
In this scenario, the teacher shares with students how the group performed and uses that to give purpose to the instructional plan they will now execute. Good practice in terms of giving purpose to students.

Conversion Example:
The written feedback on the assessment indicates which aspects of the intended learning (learning targets) the student demonstrated or failed to demonstrate in the assessment. When the teacher hands back the papers, he or she asks students to notice which of the learning targets they hit and which they missed. Then the teacher asks students to look closely at the portions of the assessment that pertained to the target(s) they did not hit to determine the cause of the miss. Was this a careless error? Did you spend too much time on other parts of the assessment and not even attempt this portion? Is this a concept you only sort of understand? Is this a concept or skill that you totally don't understand? She then asks students to report on a Google doc what support they need for each target: none, additional instruction from teacher, or a quick check-in with a peer. The teacher offers a series of short lessons on each target for those who identify they need it. She then pairs students who nailed the target with those who think a quick check-in with a peer will help them get the rest of the way there.

Connections to Proactive Characteristics:
In this example, students need to find the trend in their individual performance, identifying the underlying cause, and make a good decision about their use of time.

Routine: Addressing School Culture Issues

Common Ways of Addressing School Culture Issue:

A pattern of unwanted behavior has infected morning and lunch recess. One staff member who has reached the limit of trying to handle this bad behavior creates a behavior plan for all of the teachers to follow at recess. It involves an aggressive pattern of individual time-outs and students writing letters to parents when students repeatedly demonstrate the offending behavior. Other teachers agree to follow the plan, and all teachers share the plan with students while they are gathered as a whole group in the lunchroom. Teachers stick with this protocol until the offending behavior is a rarity.

Connections to Proactive Characteristics:

In this scenario, teachers get on the same page and more efficiently change the holistic pattern of children's behavior.

Conversion Example:

When a pattern of unwanted behavior infects morning and lunch recess, a member of the staff creates a protocol for all teachers to use with students. This protocol facilitates a discussion in which students are told this behavior in a culture is a problem, and it is their problem, and they need to identify the underlying cause for the problem, as well as identify and implement the solution. Each class has these discussions and sends one representative to a series of two to three lunch meetings facilitated by a teacher where they work to consolidate ideas from each of the class discussions into a single schoolwide plan that includes ways to monitor progress. Those students then bring the final plan back to their classes. In a quick share-out, each student shares how he or she will demonstrate commitment to the plan at recess from now on. The teacher does the same. Students and teachers hold one another accountable for follow-through on the plan by reviewing progress-monitoring information. They use that information to evaluate both the quality of the plan and the quality of their execution on a periodic ongoing basis, until measures indicate this kind of attention to this issue is no longer required.

Connections to Proactive Characteristics:

In this example, students are not just given input, but rather they are given the responsibility to fix things. They practice understanding different perspectives, analyzing a situation to really understand the root cause, and using collective focus to help individuals make different and better decisions for the community.

Again, this list is certainly not exhaustive. There are many, many, many other routine moments of school that could be redesigned to require something different of students. If you aren't sure which routines accidentally, but effectively, send kids the message that their passive compliance is the most important thing, ask your students. Ask them what parts of the day feel silliest. What parts of the day feel like something done for the sole purpose of demonstrating control? Ask them what parts of the day make them sit back and wait. Your students, even very young students, will help you find the routines that are probably most important to redesign.

When Should You Invent New Practices?

8

There are problems for which converting practice won't get the job done; this is when we need to invent. But just like the innovation process outlined in this book, we need to have a responsible and efficient way to invent. Enter the rapid prototyping design process.

There are a lot of people in a lot of different industries making use of design processes. You may have seen the *Nightline* features on the design firm IDEO as they went about the business of redesigning grocery carts to meet the needs of users. If not, you can check them out at www.youtube.com/watch?v=M66ZU2PCIcM. I also recommend checking out the more in-depth interview with David Kelley, the founder of IDEO and the d-school at Stanford (www.cbsnews.com/videos/how-to-design-breakthrough-inventions-50138327/).

David Kelley's work is really the genesis of design thinking. As someone who is an interested latecomer to this work, and certainly not an expert, I think the most distinguishing characteristic of this design process is the degree to which deep empathy for the user drives the design process. Second to that, other key characteristics include engaging people from different backgrounds and quickly prototyping and testing ideas.

To give you an idea of what Kelley and d-school are up to, I have included a brief introductory description from their website:

> The d-school is a hub for innovators at Stanford. Students and faculty in engineering, medicine, business, law, the humanities, sciences, and education find their way here to take on the world's messy problems together. Human values are at the heart of our collaborative approach. We focus on creating spectacularly transformative learning experiences. Along the way, our students develop a process for producing creative solutions to even the most complex challenges they tackle. This is the core of what we do. (http://dschool.stanford.edu/our-point-of-view/)

In addition to being potentially the coolest department at Stanford, this school has done an amazing job of making a wide range of tools and resources available for anyone to use. They also offer a range of design thinking courses, in-person and virtually, to teach people how to engage in these kinds of inventive processes. Give their site a gander and you will see just how cool their work is (http://dschool.stanford.edu/).

d-school built an activity in 2004 that every design thinking enthusiast I have met uses to introduce people to the intentions and processes of design thinking. It is called the wallet activity (https://dschool.stanford.edu/groups/designresources/wiki/4dbb2/The_Wallet_Project.html).

In this activity, people quickly (ninety minutes plus debrief) go through the whole design process used by d-school to design wallets. The process is extremely active for all participants, fast-paced, and fun. If you are thinking about doing design thinking with colleagues, I encourage you to do this activity first, for two reasons.

1. Trying to learn a new way of thinking, or a new process, is the kind of thing that requires full mental attention. If you try to learn about design thinking while working on a problem that is deeply important to you, you will tend to focus on the content of the conversation and ideas and may not learn as much about the process.

2. Taking a problem from your classroom, and putting it out there for everyone to analyze and try wild ideas to solve, is something that requires the mindset discussed in Chapter 3. In my experience, it is much easier to be in that mindset when you already know how the process is going to work. So, practicing the process with something separate from teaching may make it easier to be present, open, and humble when trying to invent ideas for your classroom.

I also encourage you to get help from local experts. If you are reading this book in any metropolitan center in America, there are probably groups of people organizing to do this kind of work. At the time of writing this book, I can identify several groups and individuals in Denver facilitating collaborative design processes to help individuals in a range of endeavors figure out their strategy or product. You may want to do a local Google search for design process, rapid prototyping, makers, or design scrimmage. I suspect you will find some local experts.

You may even be fortunate enough to have some local experts who are interested in doing this work specifically with educators. In Denver we have a few of those, and one of them has agreed to share their design process. One such group in Denver is Design Edu, led by Alex Hernandez. Here is their statement of purpose from their website (www.designedulab.org/index.html).

We are excited about the future of education and ready to stop talking and start doing. We've seen Sir Ken Robinson's TED talk, heard about Khan Academy's flipped classrooms, and read Tony Wagner's Creating Innovators. We believe innovation begins with us, with community, right here in Colorado.

After some generative work, like the wallet activity, you and your colleagues are ready to take on design of a solution. The Design Edu protocol is a good tool to use next (see Figure 8.1).

Figure 8.1 Design Edu Protocol

DESIGN EDU Feedback Protocol

Purpose: This protocol is for recurring Design EDU community events to enable education innovators to engage with each other on an ongoing basis and receive feedback and support. We think innovation starts with "doing," testing new ideas and refining them based on feedback from students and colleagues.

Format: Participants sit in a circle and engage in a 50 minute, structured, small-group conversation.

Participants:
- Educator (lead) shares an innovation they are actively working on and articulates a challenge arising from that work.
- Facilitator (volunteer) provides lightweight facilitation to mainly keep discussion on schedule.
- 6–10 Design EDU community members

Agenda

Educator frames the innovation and the challenge (5 min)

Community members gather additional information (10 min)

Community members brainstorm potential solutions to the challenge (10 min)

Educator gives feedback on ideas (3 min)

Pairs of community members prototype most promising ideas (10 min)

Pairs of community members share their ideas with educator (10 min)

Reflections from educator (3 min)

OPTIONAL SetUp / WrapUp

- *SetUp* — Each presenting educator gives 1 minute overview of their innovation to large group of community members. Community members then self-select into small groups.

- *WrapUp* — Reconvene into whole group and each presenting educator does 1 minute reflection as a wrapup and closure. Allow community members to "popcorn" any closing thoughts or reflections.

Educator frames the innovation and the challenge (5 min)

Presenting Educator Shares	*Presenting Educator Tips*	*Community Member Tips*
• School / organization context and current role • Overview and background of innovation • Challenge arising from innovation work	• Frame your challenge in a "How might we..." statement. (e.g., "How might we help my second graders become more independent readers?") • Remember, there will be 10 min of Q&A right after this where you can get into more of the details. • Don't sell. Be authentic.	• You will be brainstorming potential solutions for the educator's challenge; give yourself permission to be active during the next 50 minutes. • Identify key questions for Q&A, coming next.

Community members gather additional information (10 min)

Community Member Suggested Questions	*Presenting Educator Tips*	*Community Member Tips*
• Can you clarify... • What feedback have you received from students, colleagues (users)? • What iterations have you made with your innovation? • What have you learned so far? Where have you gotten stuck? • What other approaches have you considered?	• Keep your answers succinct so community members can get as many questions answered as possible. • Keep your answers grounded in actual experiences, feedback, and data, not opinion and speculation.	• Now is the time to get your questions answered. Brainstorming next! • Stay focused on what idea(s) the educator is testing, what feedback she has received, what she has learned, how can this help inform where to go next? • Resist the temptation to share opinions or ask leading questions. When in doubt, use the suggested questions.

Community members brainstorm potential solutions to the challenge (10 min)

Community Member Brainstorm Rules	*Presenting Educator Tips*	*Community Member Tips*
• Whole-group activity. One idea at a time. Everyone hears everyone else's ideas. • Generate as many ideas as you can, tracking them with paper, flip chart, or post-its.	• Presenting educator does not participate in or answer questions during this activity. • Listen closely so you can provide feedback next.	• Defer judgment. Get ideas out and move on to the next one. • Build on others' ideas, "Yes and..." • Don't be afraid to be wild, unrealistic!

Educator gives feedback on ideas (3 min)

Suggested Feedback from Educator	*Presenting Educator Tips*	*Community Member Tips*
• These ideas resonated with me... • I'm curious to learn more about these ideas... • These ideas give me some discomfort but you should keep pushing my thinking...	• Quickly highlight 6–10 ideas that the group might think about more. • You are trying to "rule things in," not "rule things out." • Rule things in that are both comfortable and uncomfortable. • Keep the color commentary to an absolute minimum. You want the group to keep a fresh set of eyes	• Think about any themes or patterns in the ideas generated. • Think about an idea you want to flesh out a bit more in the next activity.

Pairs of community members prototype most promising ideas (10 min)

Community Members	*Presenting Educator Tips*	*Community Member Tips*
• Organize themselves in pairs • Select an idea from the brainstorm to develop further. OK if more than one pair selects the same idea. • Develop what the next iteration of the innovation should be to address the challenge. i.e., what can the educator do on Monday and how could you quickly test to see if the idea was worth pursuing?	• Presenting educator does not participate in or answer questions during this activity. • Feel free to float to another group.	This will be your feedback to the educator which will take one of two forms. • NEXT ITERATION: Educator should be able to rapidly implement the idea and test to see if it's worth pursuing further. AND/OR • REFRAME: The current innovation doesn't get to the heart of the challenge and you might suggest a new approach.

continues

Figure 8.1 Design Edu Protocol, *cont.*

Pairs of community members share their ideas with educator (10 min)

Community Member Share Out
- Each pair has two minutes to share out the idea they developed. For example:

  "For your NEXT ITERATION, you might consider _____ to address your challenge and test it by _____."

  OR

  "If you are really trying to solve _____, you might consider REFRAMING your innovation and trying _____ such that _____."

Presenting Educator Tips
- Presenting educator listens and takes notes.

Community Member Tips
- Provide actionable, specific feedback that the educator can go work on immediately.

Reflections from educator (3 min)

Presenting Educator Shares
- Reflections from the discussion
- Ways they are thinking differently
- New things (if any) she might try
- New learnings or ideas she wants to pursue further

Presenting Educator Tips
- Allow yourself to be authentic and vulnerable.
- Sometimes you'll get some great feedback, sometimes it might be off the mark (that's OK too). Either way, share what you've learned from the feedback, the process, and/or the community.

Community Member Tips
- Admire the educator in front of you who opened up about a challenge they encountered in the work they are most passionate about.

OPTIONAL SetUp / WrapUp
- *SetUp* – Each presenting educator gives 1 minute overview of their innovation to large group of community members. Community members then self-select into small groups.
- *WrapUp* – Reconvene into whole group and each presenting educator does 1 minute reflection as a wrapup and closure. Allow community members to "popcorn" any closing thoughts or reflections.

Beyond Tools, What Does the Experience of Invention Feel Like?

At a recent Design Edu event, I asked participants to reflect on their experiences using the design process. One essential element of the experience of invention is that the disruption of invention means vulnerability on the part of the inventor, who takes a risk by putting his or her ideas out there, and on the part of the colleagues who consider the inventor's idea, who, by entertaining the inventor's idea, acknowledge that their way isn't working as well as it could.

Paul Kim, a secondary social studies teacher, tackled the problem of creating an innovative teaching lab. He said, "I was hoping to gain fresh, disruptive insight into how to affect change within a well-established faculty body. Creative ideas to push my thinking beyond common rhetoric about change, education, and teachers." When I asked him what surprised him about the conversation, here's what he said:

Hearing other educators think around my challenge informed my thinking in two ways—I need to remind myself that change is more emotional than I generally think it is, and teachers don't have enough fun for some reason. This is a part of the power of human-centered design—it provides context for pathways toward solutions.

In education, relationships are the center of the work. To be innovative educators, we have to have the courage to talk openly and honestly with our peers. That's risky and humbling. It's something we often avoid, instead choosing to focus on the children in our own classroom. But the conversation in education isn't just with the children we teach. We need to talk with our colleagues.

This means that we extend an invitation that focuses on quantity first—generating a large number of ideas—and worry about sorting them out based on interest and quality later. We listen before we act, before we evaluate for "good" or "bad." That pause is essential. It's not just an essential stance for innovation but an essential stance for teaching. We listen: we're part of a conversation and all the vulnerability and risk that true conversation entails.

If we are to innovate in ways that build public trust and drive schools forward, we have to participate in this kind of conversation with our colleagues. The potential gain is too great. Here's what Paul gained:

> My group produced about fifty ideas overall, and I have about thirty of them listed in my notes for planning purposes. The three most interesting were:
>
> 1) professional development road trips in small, socially engineered groups;
> 2) creating a curriculum design sabbatical or incorporating something like Google's 20 percent time for teachers;
> 3) designing off-the-wall, fun opportunities for faculty to remind them of the joy of teaching, knowing that the programming doesn't have to be related to teaching.
>
> I am planning to pursue all of these ideas and others from my Design Edu session over the next two years. . . . My most immediate action will be to host a Design Edu workshop at my school in November—the goal will be to try to do some fun unlearning while demonstrating the power of design thinking as a tool for both students and teachers across disciplines.

"Fun unlearning"—Paul's got a specific invitation framed for his colleagues. "Let's have fun acknowledging that we're wrong together." It's expansive, not judging. That's what we want learning to be for our students, and if we can be that way with each other, then we've passed a pretty rigorous teacher evaluation.

Calling All Teachers

9

I don't know if people ever read the conclusions of books like this. I will sheepishly acknowledge that I rarely do. I generally read through the introduction and then pull what meets my needs from the middle and don't return to read the end. Actually, as I write this I am challenged to describe how even one of my favorite books about teaching wrapped up. However, my good friend Furman said he always reads the conclusion before deciding to read a book, and that if I ever want anyone to read this book, the conclusion better be good. So, despite my lack of schema, I am going to give it a try.

This book essentially combines four ideas:

1. The twenty-first century is happening and demands that we walk away from factory school and do something different to prepare our children to be successful and happy adults.

2. Teachers need responsible ways to innovate in service of helping all students become proactive learners, professionals, and community members.

3. Teachers can both convert existing practices and invent new ways of teaching in an effort to help individual students realize their unique potential.

4. Teachers are creative, dedicated, and crafty professionals who can quickly try, fail, succeed, learn, and collectively work together to redesign the way we do school.

If you think of these four ideas relating to one another in a mathematical equation, I think it would be this one: $1 = 4(2 + 3)$. I realize this doesn't make any mathematical sense, but I think it is an equation that describes the relationships among these variables. Let me explain (see Figure 9.1).

My hope is that teachers, school leaders, and community members can come to trust this equation. That we can agree that it is time to shift the direction of innovation, so that instead of innovation being brought into the schoolhouse to be implemented with fidelity, we empower teachers to use the expertise and experiences of people outside the school to shape and inform the innovation they generate inside each of America's

Figure 9.1 Equation for Innovation: 1 = 4(2 + 3)

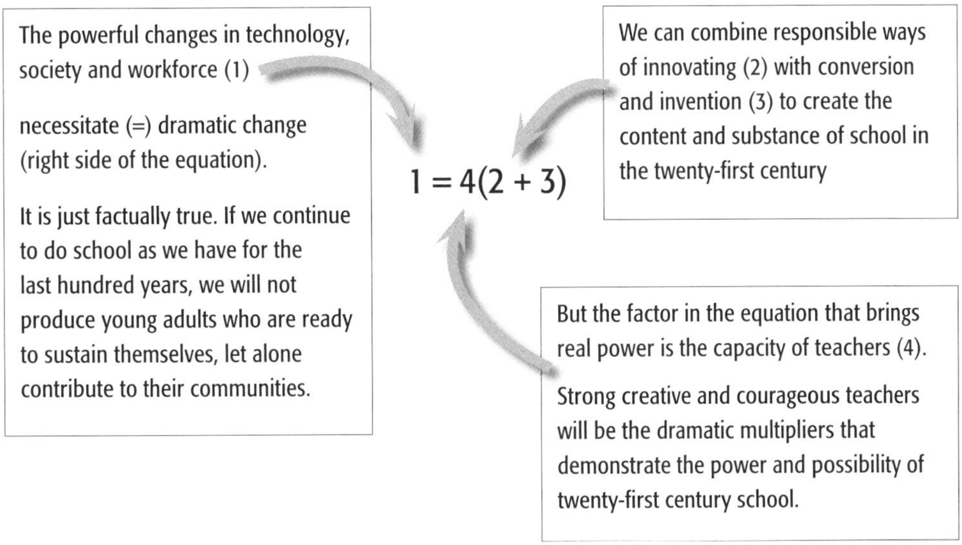

The powerful changes in technology, society and workforce (1) necessitate (=) dramatic change (right side of the equation).

It is just factually true. If we continue to do school as we have for the last hundred years, we will not produce young adults who are ready to sustain themselves, let alone contribute to their communities.

$$1 = 4(2 + 3)$$

We can combine responsible ways of innovating (2) with conversion and invention (3) to create the content and substance of school in the twenty-first century

But the factor in the equation that brings real power is the capacity of teachers (4).

Strong creative and courageous teachers will be the dramatic multipliers that demonstrate the power and possibility of twenty-first century school.

schools. We accelerate systemic learning when teachers identify problems, seek expertise to identify potential strategies, and are empowered to observe, evaluate, and revise strategies to best meet the needs of their students.

This way of working, responsible innovation applied year after year, also ensures that we don't accidentally invent the next factory, the next static view of school. This way of working commits us to continuing to shape, reshape, and redesign the American schoolhouse, so that it adjusts and evolves as quickly as the economy and society it is preparing students to enter.

So, I am calling all teachers . . .

Bring your creativity and courage.

Bring intellectual rigor and discipline.

Bring your knowledge of students and the craft of teaching.

Bring your passion for being an agent of empowerment in your communities.

Bring your friends from inside and outside the teaching community.

Bring all of that, and take on the work of bold and responsible innovation in your classroom. Take it on because you can imagine the potential impact.

Imagine working with your colleagues to use the research and good ideas of others to problem-solve and innovate within your school. Imagine feeling good about having fidelity to shared practices, language, and key ways of doing schools because you understand precisely how and why these shared approaches benefit your students. Imagine each of you giving and receiving learning and together rapidly accelerating your capacity to meet the needs of your students. Imagine continuing to innovate together, so that as technology and society continue to shift, you and your colleagues continue to produce a school experience that is relevant and valuable to your students.

Imagine how life for students who haven't presented as "naturally proactive" could be changed if school communities worked to teach them how to be proactive learners and professionals. Imagine how their transition into adult life and work will be different when they have a range of strengths, know themselves well, and have a strong sense of agency—a feeling that they can and should do something important. Imagine how neighborhoods and communities might be different if over the next generation we taught everyone to be civically engaged.

This is the power of teachers as multipliers in the equation. A small group of teachers, inventing and converting practice in their school, not only changes life outcomes for their students but can change the quality of life for everyone in their community.

So, I am calling all teachers. Bring everything you've got, and begin the work of bold innovation in your classroom.

Ready to collaborate? Feel free to copy and share the Appendix, "Responsible Innovation in Full," to get the conversation started with your colleagues or to document your own further adventures in innovation.

Appendix

Responsible Innovation Process in Full

Phase, Time, and Tasks of Education Innovation

Phase of the Work	Estimated Timeframe	Tasks
Identification	2–4 hours	• Identify the thing you want to make better (the problem). • Identify the idea (strategy) with maximum potential to solve the problem.
Planning	8–12 hours	• Articulate the rationale that supports that idea. • Determine what results implementing that idea should yield in the very short term. • Determine how to gather information about those results. • Map out implementation steps, and build whatever tools you need to try it out.
Implementation and Monitoring	Between 2 and 10 weeks	• Try it. • Gather information and monitor results.
Analysis	2 hours	• Evaluate results with colleagues.
Impact	Timing depends on result	Based on results do one of these three things: 1. If results are bad, analyze the work and rationale to understand why it failed, and never do it or other things with those bad premises again. Share that learning with your colleagues to prevent them from the same failure. 2. If the results are mixed, analyze to understand what worked and didn't. Revisit rationale to see if it still holds up. Try to fix it and repeat the process. 3. If the results were positive, figure out how to share it with your colleagues so they can benefit from your smart ideas and good work.

Identification Tools

Why, why, why?

What is the problem? What do you want to improve?

	Why is the problem happening?
Why are those things happening?	The answer might be . . .
Why are those things happening?	The answer might be . . .
Why are those things happening?	The answer might be . . .

So, the most basic problem here is

Corroborate

So, the most basic problem here is

What data/information could corroborate or debunk problem identification?	Did examining that information corroborate or debunk problem identification?
Who do you know with expertise that could corroborate or debunk problem identification?	Did the colleague corroborate or debunk problem identification?

Identify Strategy

Once there is a list of possible strategies, it is time to place bets and decide which one to implement first. In some cases, this can be a pretty quick process. If there are two or three ideas competing for best idea, and each of them is aimed squarely at a problem that has been identified and corroborated—there may not need to be a lot of science in determining which to try first.

Is there a strategy that naturally rises to the top for you? If so—identify that strategy here.

_____

_____

If what to try first isn't readily apparent, list your top five (or fewer) strategy ideas in the table below. Then use the questions provided to help you compare strategies and determine with which strategy to begin.

Strategy 1:

Strategy 2:

Strategy 3:

Strategy 4:

Strategy 5:

Questions to Consider

- Which option is easiest for you to try?

- Which option has the fewest, or easiest to mitigate, possible negative risks associated with it?

- Which option do your colleagues think has the greatest potential?

- Which option do your colleagues think they would also like to try?

- Which option requires the fewest resources to deliver with quality?

- Would one of the options inherently produce data that would help you evaluate effectiveness?

- Does one of these options align more closely to the shared values and mission of your school?

- Which option does your well-informed gut say will have the greatest impact?

Planning Tools

Articulate the Rationale That Supports the Winning Idea Identified in Step 1

This should be something you can do quickly, as you have deeply explored the rationale in step 1. It is important, though, to write it down clearly and concisely. This will help you synthesize why you are planning; it will also help you more easily explain to your students, families, and colleagues what you are trying and why.

Determine What Results Implementing Those Ideas Should Yield in the Very Short Term and Determine How to Gather Information About Those Results

Left Column: As you imagine beginning to implement your strategy, what do you think you will be able to see in the first few weeks to help you determine whether this strategy is working or not? One of the promises of using the responsible innovation process is that failure will be spotted and addressed quickly. Before implementing, it is essential to determine how you will know quickly if the strategy is working.

Right Column: Sometimes tools or plans with colleagues will be necessary to actually collect the information needed to evaluate whether the strategy is working. Before digging into detailed planning or implementation, take a moment to identify what work may need to be done to collect the required information. Consider the following questions . . .

- Do you need to create an observation tool?

- Will you be able to observe for these things yourself, or do you need help from colleagues?

- Could you create a student reflection tool? How frequently do you want to ask them to notice whether the strategy is helping them in the way you intended?

- Could you create a pre and post student survey?

- What opportunities are coming to see impact on in-class assessments or participation in interim assessments?

- What kinds of changes do you think you will see first? What kinds of changes do you not expect to see right away, but you do expect to see later in the timeframe in which you plan to implement?

Data Collection grid: *Things I can observe, hear, or analyze along the way that would indicate that my strategy is working*

Observable student behaviors	I might observe students . . .	I can best collect observation data for each of these in the following way:
What students may say if the strategy is working	My students may say things like . . .	I can best collect their perceptions by . . .
Changes that can be observed by examining student work	I might see . . .	I can gather and analyze that data by . . .

Plan Steps and Build Whatever Tools Are Needed to Try It Out and Gather Information About Results

Step# _____		Estimated Timing:
Me	**Learning Target** •	**Teacher Actions** •
My Students	**Learning Target** •	**Student Actions** •

Indicators of Success:

I might observe students . . .

My students may say things like . . .

Student work may change to . . .

Tools and Resources Needed:

Monitoring Notes:

References

Aud, S., S. Wilkinson-Flicker, P. Kristapovich, A. Rathbun, X. Wang, and J. Zhang. 2013a. *The Condition of Education, 2013* (NCES 2013-037). http://nces.ed.gov /programs/coe/indicator_coj.asp. Washington, DC: U.S. Department of Education, National Center for Education Statistics.

Aud, S., S. Wilkinson-Flicker, P. Kristapovich, A. Rathbun, X. Wang, and J. Zhang, J. 2013b. *The Condition of Education, 2013* (NCES 2013-037). http://nces.ed.gov /programs/coe/indicator_coi.asp. Washington, DC: U.S. Department of Education, National Center for Education Statistics.

Bryant, A. 2013. "In Head-Hunting, Big Data May Not Be Such a Big Deal." *New York Times*, June 19. www.nytimes.com/2013/06/20/business/in-head-hunting-big -data-may-not-be-such-a-big-deal.html?pagewanted =2&pagewanted=all&_r=1&

Dweck, C. 2006. *Mindset*. New York: Random House.

Friedman, T. L. 2013. "Need a Job? Invent It." *New York Times*, March 30. www .nytimes.com/2013/03/31/opinion/sunday/friedman-need-a-job-invent-it.html? _r=1&

Kaushik, A. 2008. "10 Insights from 11 Months of Working at Google."

Occam's Razor, February 11 (blog). www.kaushik.net/avinash/10-insights-from -11-months-of-working-at-google/

National Center for Education Statistics. 2013. The Nation's Report Card: Trends in Academic Progress, 2012 (NCES 2013–456). http://nces.ed.gov /nationsreportcard/subject/publications/main2012/pdf/2013456.pdf. Washington, DC: National Center for Education Statistics, Institute of Education Sciences, U.S. Department of Education.

Roundtable, Inc. 2001. *School: The Story of American Public Education*. PBS Documentary. www.pbs.org/kcet/publicschool/roots_in_history/testing _timeline1.html

Snyder, T. D., and S. A. Dillow. 2012. *Digest of Education Statistics, 2011* (NCES 2012 -001). http://nces.ed.gov/programs/digest/d11/tables/dt11_345.asp Washington, DC: National Center for Education Statistics, Institute of Education Sciences, U.S. Department of Education.

Stiggins, R. J., J. A. Arter, J. Chappuis, and S. Chappuis. 2006. *Classroom Assessment for Student Learning: Doing It Right—Using It Well.* Upper Saddle River, NJ: Prentice Hall.

Vedder, R., C. Denhart, and J. Robe. 2013. *Why Are Recent College Graduates Underemployed? University Enrollments and Labor-Market Realities.* centerforcollegeaffordability.org/research/studies/underemployment-of-college -graduates. Washington, DC: Center for College Affordability and Productivity.

Watson, Stephanie. 2008. "How Public Schools Work," February 13. HowStuffWorks. com. http://people.howstuffworks.com/public-schools.htm 08.

Zhao, Y. 2012. *World Class Learners.* Thousand Oaks, CA: Corwin.